Created Male and Female

Created Male and Female

Terrance Randall Wardlaw Jr.

Foreword by David M. Howard Jr.

WIPF & STOCK · Eugene, Oregon

CREATED MALE AND FEMALE

Wipf & Stock
An Imprint of Wipf and Stock Publishers
199 W. 8th Ave., Suite 3
Eugene, OR 97401

www.wipfandstock.com

PAPERBACK ISBN: 978-1-7252-8464-7
HARDCOVER ISBN: 978-1-7252-8460-9
EBOOK ISBN: 978-1-7252-8465-4

01/18/21

δόξα ἐν ὑψίστοις θεῷ

וַיֹּ֣אמֶר אֱלֹהִ֗ים נַֽעֲשֶׂ֥ה אָדָ֛ם בְּצַלְמֵ֖נוּ כִּדְמוּתֵ֑נוּ וְיִרְדּוּ֩ בִדְגַ֨ת הַיָּ֜ם וּבְע֣וֹף
הַשָּׁמַ֗יִם וּבַבְּהֵמָה֙ וּבְכָל־הָאָ֔רֶץ וּבְכָל־הָרֶ֖מֶשׂ הָֽרֹמֵ֥שׂ עַל־הָאָֽרֶץ:
וַיִּבְרָ֨א אֱלֹהִ֤ים | אֶת־הָֽאָדָם֙ בְּצַלְמ֔וֹ בְּצֶ֥לֶם אֱלֹהִ֖ים בָּרָ֣א אֹת֑וֹ זָכָ֥ר
וּנְקֵבָ֖ה בָּרָ֥א אֹתָֽם:

Then God said, "Let us make man in our image, after our likeness.
And let them have dominion over the fish of the sea and over the
birds of the heavens and over the livestock and over all the earth and
over every creeping thing that creeps on the earth." So God created
man in his own image, in the image of God he created him; male and
female he created them.

—GENESIS 1:26–27 (ESV)

Contents

Contents

List of Tables

Foreword

I HAVE KNOWN TERRY Wardlaw since 2010, when he invited me to teach a week-long seminar for Bible translators on hermeneutics and exegesis. It was an incredible blessing to be among front-line workers for the gospel in an often-difficult environment, helping them to integrate their linguistic expertise with solid principles for Bible translation and interpretation. I got to know Terry as a careful translator and scholar in his own right, and also as one who loved the Lord, loved the church, and loved the people of the land where he worked.

It is out of his love for God and the church that this book has been birthed. Terry's concern for right interpretation has led him to address the issues of male-female relations, since he has closely watched the egalitarian-complementarian battles and laments what he sees as an abandonment of biblical authority and/or a distortion of key biblical texts by leading egalitarians.

But, this is not simply a rehash of traditional arguments, which ground has been well trodden in the last four to five decades. Rather, Terry comes at the issues from a fresh (and unexpected) perspective: through the lens of creation ethics. Most of us think of ecology—"creation care"—when considering the creation mandate in Genesis 1:26–28. But, as Terry points out, creation ethics encompass more than that. Included are "differentiation as male and female, filling the earth with offspring, and the sanctification of the seventh day (Gen 1:26–2:3)."

Because of this, Terry explores the issues of male-female roles and relationships in the Bible through this distinctive lens, and he adds fresh perspectives on the issues. This is a book well worth reading.

DAVID M. HOWARD JR.
Professor of Old Testament
Bethlehem College and Seminary
Minneapolis, Minnesota

Professor of Old Testament, *Emeritus*
Bethel Seminary (Bethel University)
St. Paul, Minnesota

July 6, 2020

List of Abbreviations

AGJU	Arbeiten zur Geschichte des antiken Judentums und des Urchristentums
ANF	*Ante-Nicene Fathers*. Edited by Alexander Roberts and James Donaldson. 1885–1887. 10 vols. Reprint, Peabody, MA: Hendrickson, 1994.
BDAG	Walter Bauer, F. W. Danker, W. F. Arndt, and F. W. Gingrich. *A Greek-English Lexicon of the New Testament and other Early Christian Literature*. 3rd ed. Chicago: University of Chicago Press, 1999.
BibInt	*Biblical Interpretation*
CC	Continental Commentaries
ESV	English Standard Version
GHAT	Göttingen Handkommentar zum Alten Testament
GKC	W. Gesenius, E. Kautzsch, and A. E. Cowley. *Gesenius' Hebrew Grammar*. 2nd. ed. Oxford: Clarendon, 1910.
HALOT	Ludwig Koehler, Walter Baumgartner, and Johann Jakob Stamm. *The Hebrew and Aramaic Lexicon of the Old Testament*. Translated and edited by M. E. J. Richardson. 2 vols. Leiden: Brill, 2001.
JBMW	*Journal of Biblical Manhood and Womanhood*
Joüon	Paul Joüon and T. Muraoka. *A Grammar of Biblical Hebrew*. 2 vols. Subsidia Biblica 14/I. Rome: Pontificio Istituto Biblico, 2003.

LXX	Septuagint (Greek translation of the Hebrew Bible, dating c. 250 BC)
MT	Masoretic Text (Hebrew Bible)
NASB	New American Standard Bible
NET	New English Translation
NIGTC	New International Greek Text Commentary
NIV	New International Version
NKJV	New King James Version
NLT	New Living Translation
NPNF	*Nicene and Post-Nicene Fathers.* Series 1: Edited by Philip Schaff. 1886–1889. 14 vols. Series 2: Edited by Philip Schaff and Henry Wace. 1890–1900. 14 vols. Reprint, Peabody, MA: Hendrickson, 1994.
NRSV	New Revised Standard Version
NT	New Testament
OBT	Overtures to Biblical Theology
OT	Old Testament
SubBi	*Subsidia Biblica*
Tg.	Targum (Aramaic translation of the Old Testament)
Vg.	Latin Vulgate
IBHS	Bruce Waltke and M. O'Connor. *An Introduction to Biblical Hebrew Syntax.* Winona Lake, IN: Eisenbrauns, 1990.

Chapter 1

Ethics and the Climax of Creation

MANY IMMEDIATELY TUMBLE TO the topic of ecology when considering the ethical implications of creation in Genesis 1. Conceived
more broadly, the category of creation ethics does indeed encompass the issue of human dominion over all living things and care
for the earth, and yet it also includes differentiation as male and
female, filling the earth with offspring, and the sanctification of the
seventh day (Gen 1:26—2:3).[1] In particular, the present study will
focus upon ethics associated with the creation of and the distinction between man and woman. Since the creation of humanity on
day six occurs within the literary climax of the introductory materials to the canon of Scripture, the neglect of the church catholic
to recognize and prophetically declare the ethics of sexual differentiation in contemporary society seems puzzling. Indeed, we
shall observe that St. Paul recognized the significance of day six in
Genesis 1:26–31, as well as the narrative of Genesis 2, and grounded his understanding of the identity and roles of men and women
precisely in these texts.[2] Therefore, the institutional church's neglect and, at times, contradiction of created sexual differentiation

1. Frame, *Christian Life*, 202–3. For a more recent general treatment of ethics, see Grudem, *Christian Ethics*.

2. Paul's grounding of ethics in Torah has been observed in Tomson, *Paul
and the Jewish Law*; Witherington, *Paul's Narrative Thought World*; Rosner,
Paul, Scripture and Ethics.

overturns one of the main emphases of creation as God revealed it and as the early church received it. As noted by Frame, creation ordinances form the basic law of human existence. Because they are grounded in creation rather than in the Mosaic covenant, it remains unlikely that God would overturn or significantly modify these ordinances in the course of history.[3]

But to the point. In reflecting upon the present day, it remains axiomatic for a church steeped in Western culture that men and women are created equal, and that patriarchy entered only with the fall. Therefore, egalitarians argue that in Christ no role distinction remains between the two, women should serve alongside men in leadership roles and teaching positions, and no hierarchy remains within marriage. Anything less is fallen, repressive, opposed to the Gospel, smacks of sexism, and leads to domestic abuse.[4] Moreover, some egalitarians argue that if the New Testament requires wives

3. Frame, *Christian Life*, 203.

4. Byrd, *Recovering from Biblical Manhood and Womanhood*; cf. Naselli, "Does Anyone Need to Recover from Biblical Manhood and Womanhood?"; Ruth Tucker, *Black and White Bible*; cf. Kassian, Review of *Black and White Bible*. For earlier egalitarian presentations, see Scanzoni and Hardesty, *All We're Meant to Be*; Jewett, *Man as Male and Female*; Jewett, *Ordination of Women*; Spencer, *Beyond the Curse*; Bilezikian, *Beyond Sex Roles*; Tucker, *Women in the Maze*; Groothuis, *Feminist Bogeywoman*; Groothuis, *Good News for Women*; Pierce and Groothuis, *Discovering Biblical Equality*; Spencer et al., *Global Voices on Biblical Equality*; Payne, *Man and Woman, One in Christ*; Riswold, *Feminism and Christianity*; Hunt and Neu, *New Feminist Christianity*; Pierce, *Partners in Marriage and Ministry*; Tucker, *Dynamic Women of the Bible*; Murphy and Starling, *Gender Conversation*; Hung, "Defending My Daughters"; Miller, "Misinterpreting 'Head' Can Perpetuate Abuse." Cf. Moore, "O.J. Simpson Is Not a Complementarian"; Piper, "Clarifying Words on Wife Abuse"; Pierre, "Overlooked Help." For a response to Pierce and Groothuis, see *JBMW* 10.1 (2005). For one account of the rise of women in ministry within evangelical circles, see Hassey, *No Time for Silence*. For key works on feminist hermeneutics, see Trible, *God and the Rhetoric of Sexuality*; Trible, *Texts of Terror*; Schüssler Fiorenza, *But She Said*; Schüssler Fiorenza, *In Memory of Her*; Schüssler Fiorenza, *Wisdom Ways*; Schüssler Fiorenza, *Bread Not Stone*; Ruether, *Sexism and God-Talk*. For the trajectory of religious feminism, see Ruether, *Gaia and God*; Ruether, *Womanguides*; Ruether, *Goddesses and the Divine Feminine*; Kidd, *Dance of the Dissident Daughter*; cf. Spencer, *Goddess Revival*. For one view of secular feminism, see Baumgardner and Richards, *Manifesta*.

to submit to their husbands, then it also legitimates slavery and requires government by kings.[5] Therefore, so the argument goes, we cannot absolutize the culture in which the Bible was written.[6]

Traditionalists hardly help this perception. Appeals in previous generations to tradition and broad theological considerations, rather than to the contextual meaning of the very words of Scripture, were doomed to failure. For example, C. S. Lewis in the Anglican context argued against priestesses in the church. He argued chiefly from tradition, broad theological themes, and *ad hoc* observations which would not be granted today, and he never once appealed to 2 Timothy 2:8–15.[7] The grounding of tradition upon the teaching of Scripture had been forgotten, the authority of holy writ eclipsed. Thus, the fields were prepared for sowing the claim that traditional views regarding the roles of men and women in the church were based on nothing more than cultural convention.[8]

However, following in the wake of other complementarian writers, the present discussion first intends to present Scripture itself in order to establish the cumulative argument that the coherent doctrine of New Testament complementarian teaching derives from the inspired and authoritative application of Old Testament exegesis rather than from the culture in which the Bible was written.[9] Accordingly, New Testament teaching founded upon creation

5. Mollenkott, *Women, Men, and the Bible*, 73–87; Webb, *Slaves, Women and Homosexuals*; cf. Knight, *Role Relationship of Men and Women*, 9–15. Regarding the issue of hermeneutics, see Appendices 2 and 3, as well as the cited references, in Köstenberger and Köstenberger, *God's Design for Man and Woman*, 321–53.

6. McKnight, *Blue Parakeet*, 145–207.

7. Lewis, "Priestesses in the Church?"

8. Groothuis, *Women Caught in the Conflict*.

9. For thorough treatments of biblical teaching on the roles of men and women, application, and a description of egalitarianism and the manner in which it leads the church down the path of error, see Knight, *Role Relationship of Men and Women*; Bordwine, *Pauline Doctrine of Male Headship*; Grudem, *Biblical Foundations for Manhood and Womanhood*; Grudem and Rainey, *Pastoral Leadership for Manhood and Womanhood*; Grudem, *Evangelical Feminism and Biblical Truth*; Grudem, *Evangelical Feminism: A New Path?*; Grudem, *Countering the Claims of Evangelical Feminism*; Köstenberger, *God's*

ordinances hermeneutically assumes universal validity and authority since inspired exegesis and application derives from God's revelation rather than from cultural standards, the fall, or an abrogated Mosaic covenant. Second, during the course of discussion this study seeks to glean contextual insights from Scripture regarding the roles and responsibilities of elect men and women in marriage and society. Contemporary egalitarianism—or rather Christian feminism—speaks stridently in monovocal fashion across much of the institutional church, many Bible college faculties, seminaries, mission agencies, and Christian publishers, whereas Scripture teaches the opposite viewpoint most baldly in passages such as 2 Timothy 2:8–15.[10] Accordingly, we shall begin by examining Genesis 1–3, key passages from the Historical Books, and key New Testament epistolary texts. The present discussion assumes the inspiration, authority, inerrancy, and clarity of Scripture in each of these passages, and recognizes that it is precisely the doctrine of Scripture which is at stake when evangelical Christians discuss created roles.[11] For if the plain sense of Scripture may be twisted to fit a feminist agenda, then all sense of objective meaning has been lost and Scripture may be co-opted in support of anything. Third, this investigation seeks to

---

Design for Man and Woman.

10. Some egalitarians acknowledge that Jesus and the human authors of Scripture were not egalitarian: Elliott, "Jesus Was Not an Egalitarian"; Elliott, "Jesus Movement Was Not Egalitarian"; Corley, *Women and the Historical Jesus.*

11. For example, Virginia Mollenkott directly attacks Scripture's witness of its inspiration, authority, and inerrancy, as described by B. B. Warfield, when she condones Paul K. Jewett's assertion that Paul contradicts himself on the subject of women, and when she refers to "Paul's rationalization for the female subordination that was standard in his culture" and finds "the passages are distorted by the human instrument, yet they are instructive in showing us an honest man in conflict with himself" (*Women, Men, and the Bible,* 85–86; cf. Warfield, *Revelation and Inspiration,* 1:3–112, 169–226, 395–425). As described by Warfield, human authorship does not entail error. If Paul contradicts himself, then those who follow Mollenkott's hermeneutic must dispense with inerrancy, and in turn depart from conservative evangelicalism. Moreover, if statements on women cannot be trusted, how may those who take this approach trust the authority of statements regarding atonement and justification? This issue goes straight to the heart of the reliability and the clarity of Scripture in a direct attack on the traditional evangelical doctrine of Scripture.

discover the patristic interpretation of key biblical texts. Since some writers and bloggers refer to patristic literature and intimate the fathers agreed with or taught egalitarianism, the actual statements of patristic writers will be summarized and quoted for key passages in order for readers to see for themselves the beliefs taught by the church fathers. These orthodox teachers remain perhaps one of the most misquoted sources in the attempt of postmoderns to rewrite church history in their own image on issues ranging from creation and the historicity of Adam, to the nature of marriage. This appeal to patristic literature is not toward the end of an argument from tradition, but rather seeks to discover how the early church understood and applied Scripture. Reception history functions as a corrective for the historical, cultural, and linguistic distance of modernity and postmodernity. Otherwise, the temptation looms large to assume this generation's "common sense" has been maintained in all times and places as self-evidently true.[12]

From the outset, the present author acknowledges that more must be said regarding the biblical responsibilities of redeemed men in treating women with dignity and respect. However, the present work limits its scope to defining the nature and contextual meaning of the anthropological theme of man and woman in Scripture in response to the increasing influence of evangelical feminism and the questionable exegetical practices wielded in its support. The implications of the present approach lead to a call for men to grow in Christlikeness. This call, in conjunction with a serious and rigorous application of passages such as 1 Corinthians 13, Ephesians 5:21–33, and Philippians 2:3–4, entails the inculcation of a culture within the church which does not tolerate demeaning statements toward women, domestic abuse, the use of pornography, or any behavior which supports the industry of sex trafficking. Ironically, as evangelical feminists attempt to better the plight of women, the ensuing feminization of the institutional church marginalizes men, many of whom want nothing to do with neutered godliness. Men vote with their feet, and the church exhibits a diminishing influence on male culture with each passing year. Men behave badly and throw off all

12. Lewis, "On the Reading of Old Books=."

constraint rather than submitting to the Word and the Spirit subsequent to regeneration. Inwardly craving significance and respect, men misguidedly attempt to satisfy their lusts with work, recreation, and illicit sexual gratification. Many women long to be loved faithfully and cherished, and instead our culture lifts high a male agenda and male characteristics as the ultimate for female achievement. The Bible speaks to this situation.

Moreover, the erasure of characteristic male and female identity within the church silences the church's prophetic declaration to the nations regarding created and blessed sexual differences. The outworking of secular feminism within Western culture has resulted in the rise of the LGBTQ movement and its universal advocacy in the pulpit of mainstream media.[13] The ideologically driven egalitarian movement hamstrings the church and prevents it from presenting a well reasoned and articulate response with a unified voice in the hope of influencing Western culture for the good.

Finally, the present discussion is not intended as a comprehensive defense of complementarianism, which maintains adherence to a straightforward and contextual reading of 2 Timothy 2:8–15 and other passages, nor is it intended as a refutation of every nuance or novel argument presented by contemporary egalitarians, who argue no biblical mandate exists for the distinction in roles between men and women. Rather, this discussion aims toward the more modest goal of presenting a straightforward and sequential reading of passages from Scripture relevant to creation as male and female. Although many detailed treatments exist of aspects of this debate, no comprehensive and reasonably succinct summary presentation of scriptural teaching on created differentiation remains readily available for the educated layman, pastor, or seminary student. This book intends to fill this gap, while avoiding more detailed and complex argumentation obscuring the overall thrust of Scripture.

With these thoughts in mind, we now turn to a discussion of the creation, fall, and redemption of men and women in biblical Law (Genesis through Deuteronomy).

13. DeRouchie, "Confronting the Transgender Storm"; Parnell and Strachan, *Designed for Joy*; Strachan and Peacock, *Grand Design*.

Chapter 2

Old Testament Foundational Texts

The Pentateuch

THE ACCOUNTS OF THE creation of man and woman and of their relationship and fall occur at the outset of the biblical narrative (Gen 1:26–28; 2:4—3:4). Therefore, the placement of biblical materials suggests the centrality of properly understanding the identity of men and women for life within God's created kingdom. Some argue that whereas Christology, the Trinity, and atonement are central themes, the roles of men and women are not. Therefore, supposedly, those with a strong conviction about the biblical view of the created roles of men and women should not expend such energy quibbling over ancillary issues. However, this placement of the distinction between male and female at the climax of creation and at the beginning of the Christian canon elevates its prominence—if we take Scripture seriously on its own terms and in context. Therefore, we now proceed with a straightforward reading of creation in Genesis 1 and the relationship between man and woman described in Genesis 2–3.[1]

---

1. Cf. Hess, "Equality With and Without Innocence," 96–109; Giles, "Genesis of Equality"; Giles, "Genesis of Confusion."

Created Male and Female

1. Genesis 1 and the Distinction between Man and Woman

The creation account in Genesis 1:1—2:3 climaxes with the creation
of mankind on day six (1:26–31). This account begins in Genesis
1:26 with God creating mankind in his own image and giving man
dominion over fish, birds, livestock, and every creeping thing.[2]

Genesis 1:26
וַיֹּ֣אמֶר אֱלֹהִ֗ים נַֽעֲשֶׂ֥ה אָדָ֛ם בְּצַלְמֵ֖נוּ כִּדְמוּתֵ֑נוּ וְיִרְדּוּ֩ בִדְגַ֨ת הַיָּ֜ם וּבְע֣וֹף הַשָּׁמַ֗יִם וּבַבְּהֵמָה֙ וּבְכָל־הָאָ֔רֶץ וּבְכָל־הָרֶ֖מֶשׂ הָרֹמֵ֥שׂ עַל־הָאָֽרֶץ׃
And God said, "Let us make man in our image, after our likeness. And let them have dominion over the fish of the sea and over the birds of the heavens and over the livestock and over all the earth and over every creeping thing that creeps on the earth."[3]

Table 2.1. The text of Genesis 1:26

At this point in the narrative a division between male and female
is not specified. Moreover, dominion over creation likewise applies
to all of mankind.

However, the next verse, Genesis 1:27, introduces the distinction between male and female.

Genesis 1:27
וַיִּבְרָ֨א אֱלֹהִ֤ים ׀ אֶת־הָֽאָדָם֙ בְּצַלְמ֔וֹ בְּצֶ֥לֶם אֱלֹהִ֖ים בָּרָ֣א אֹת֑וֹ זָכָ֥ר וּנְקֵבָ֖ה בָּרָ֥א אֹתָֽם׃
⌜So God created man in his own image, in the image of God he created him; male and female he created them.

Table 2.2. The text of Genesis 1:27

Creation as male and female indicates a sexual distinction which
opposes contemporary attempts in popular Western culture to erase
the boundaries in order to establish the fluidity between the sexes.
Although the full implications of this distinction are not spelled out

2. For a more detailed treatment of creation in the image of God, as well
as references to further literature, see Gentry, "Humanity as the Divine Image
in Genesis 1:26–28."

3. Unless otherwise indicated, all English Scripture quotations are taken
from the ESV.

8

within these verses, the Bible elsewhere indicates its fuller significance. Moreover, this verse indicates that the division between male and female is part of the created order prior to the fall in Genesis 3. Therefore, biblically speaking, the distinction between male and female is not to be erased. In fact, to attempt to erase this distinction willfully opposes the intent of the Creator, who similarly distinguished between light and darkness, as well as the waters and dry land (Gen 1:2–25). The Genesis narrative goes on to demonstrate that the failure to maintain created boundaries and distinctions results in a reversal of creation with the unleashing of the waters of chaos (Gen 6–9).

In fact, following the statement that God created man male and female, the divine blessing and the decree of human dominion are given (Gen 1:28–30). This order suggests there is a blessing in the distinction between male and female, and that a right ordering of creation maintains this distinction. Furthermore, this distinction is blessed for the purpose of fruitfulness. God created male and female with differences, and the blessing indicates the goal to be that of bearing children in order to fill the earth. This creation blessing therefore speaks over and against any worldview or ideology standing in opposition to fruitfulness and bearing children.

Created Male and Female

Genesis 1:28–30
28 וַיְבָרֶךְ אֹתָם֮ אֱלֹהִים֒ וַיֹּאמֶר לָהֶם אֱלֹהִים פְּרוּ וּרְבוּ וּמִלְאוּ אֶת־הָאָרֶץ וְכִבְשֻׁהָ וּרְדוּ בִּדְגַת הַיָּם וּבְעוֹף הַשָּׁמַיִם וּבְכָל־חַיָּה הָרֹמֶשֶׂת עַל־הָאָרֶץ: 29 וַיֹּאמֶר אֱלֹהִים הִנֵּה נָתַתִּי לָכֶם אֶת־כָּל־עֵשֶׂב ׀ זֹרֵעַ זֶרַע אֲשֶׁר עַל־פְּנֵי כָל־הָאָרֶץ וְאֶת־כָּל־הָעֵץ אֲשֶׁר־בּוֹ פְרִי־עֵץ זֹרֵעַ זָרַע לָכֶם יִהְיֶה לְאָכְלָה: 30 וּלְכָל־חַיַּת הָאָרֶץ וּלְכָל־עוֹף הַשָּׁמַיִם וּלְכֹל ׀ רוֹמֵשׂ עַל־הָאָרֶץ אֲשֶׁר־בּוֹ נֶפֶשׁ חַיָּה אֶת־כָּל־יֶרֶק עֵשֶׂב לְאָכְלָה וַיְהִי־כֵן: 31 וַיַּרְא אֱלֹהִים אֶת־כָּל־אֲשֶׁר עָשָׂה וְהִנֵּה־טוֹב מְאֹד וַיְהִי־עֶרֶב וַיְהִי־בֹקֶר יוֹם הַשִּׁשִּׁי:

28 And God blessed them. And God said to them, "Be fruitful and multiply and fill the earth and subdue it, and have dominion over the fish of the sea and over the birds of the heavens and over every living thing that moves on the earth." 29 And God said, "Behold, I have given you every plant yielding seed that is on the face of all the earth, and every tree with seed in its fruit. You shall have them for food. 30 And to every beast of the earth and to every bird of the heavens and to everything that creeps on the earth, everything that has the breath of life, I have given every green plant for food." And it was so. 31 And God saw everything that he had made, and behold, it was very good. And there was evening and there was morning, the sixth day.

Table 2.3. The text of Genesis 1:28–30

Directly on the heels of the distinction follows the climactic decree, "And God saw everything that he had made, and behold, it was very good" (Gen 1:31a). Thus, differentiation for the purpose of bearing children is good in the eyes of the Creator. This passage therefore speaks with authority and corrects any worldview which threatens this order, whether it be the empty materialism requiring both members of a couple to slave for possessions, or whether it be the feminist goal of egalitarian work opportunity and achievement in order to find fulfillment outside the home. The muddling of created roles results in the unleashing of chaos in opposition to the Creator's purpose of growing families and fruitfully filling the earth.

Therefore, one of the main points made at the outset of biblical narrative is that God created a distinction between male and female, and there is both blessing and a created purpose of bearing children inherent within it. Moreover, God deems this distinction to be "very good." Conversely, erasing this boundary loses the divine blessing, loses dominion over the created order, and loses the highest divine approval. Situated within the larger

10

narrative context of Genesis, the failure to maintain this separation unleashes the waters of chaos (Gen 1:2). Chaos lurks at the ready whenever humanity casts aside the boundaries of creation and the moral order of the covenants (Gen 6–8; 18–19).

2. Relationship Depicted in Genesis 2–3

Genesis 2:4—3:24 adds to the distinction between male and female in Genesis 1:27 by depicting the roles of male and female positively before the fall, and then negatively during and after the fall. Whereas Genesis 1:1—2:3 concerns creation by separation, order, and the reign of God, Genesis 2:4—3:24 focuses upon the intended roles of men and women, as well as the violation of these created roles in the fall.

Within Genesis 2:5–14 the dry land is watered, the Lord God forms man from the dust of the earth, God breathes the breath of life into him, and plants the garden in Eden with the tree of life, with the tree of the knowledge of good and evil, and with the four rivers. The Lord God appoints man to work and to keep the garden of Eden, and permits the man to eat of any tree of the garden except the tree of the knowledge of good and evil (Gen 2:15–17). Then in Genesis 2:18 the Lord God declares that it is not good for man to be alone, and so purposes to "make him a helper fit for him" (ESV) or, according to the Authorized Version, "a suitable helpmate." The Lord God forms every beast of the field and bird of the heavens, brings them to the man to be named, and then none of them is found to be a suitable helper (Gen 2:18–20). Thereupon, "the Lord God caused a deep sleep to fall upon the man, and while he slept took one of his ribs and closed up its place with flesh. And the rib that the Lord God had taken from the man he made into a woman and brought her to the man" (Gen 2:21–22).

In looking to the overall narrative of Genesis 2, one first observes the Lord God created a woman for the man. This defines the prototypical and blessed marriage relationship. Following the thrust of this narrative, the marriage of male and female derives from creation, whereas the LGBTQ ideology of male marrying male, female marrying female, and all other various blurred combinations do not fall within the bounds of the Creator's purpose. Regardless of the rhetoric employed to the contrary, no illicit union conforms to the Creator's intended order. Second, the creation of Eve for Adam implies the Lord God intends one man and one wife for life within the kingdom. This ideal does not allow for marrying one person at a time, and changing marriage partners periodically following divorce. God focused the narrative on Adam and Eve for a purpose, and God did not create a community of potential partners so that Adam and Eve could move on to someone else once they grew tired of one another, disagreed over something, or focused on their incompatibilities. Rather, Adam was to keep Eve close to his heart, and Eve was created in order to help Adam to be fruitful. Devotion to one another and faithfulness to their created roles endured for life, and it is precisely these roles which have been jettisoned in many sectors of the church today.

Discussions of the roles of men and women hinge upon the meaning of the phrase "a helper fit for him" (Gen 2:18, 20). Early translators rendered the Hebrew phrase עֵזֶר כְּנֶגְדּוֹ (ezer kenegdo) as "a helper suitable/corresponding to/like himself" (LXX: βοηθὸν κατ᾽ αὐτόν, boēthon kat' auton; Tg.: סְמָךְ בְּקִבְלֵיהּ, semakh kheqivleh; Vg.: adiutorium similem sui) from 250 BC through the fourth century AD. English translations of the Bible render this phrase "a helper corresponding to him," "a helper suitable for him," or "a suitable helpmate." Traditional Jewish commentary on this phrase capitalizes upon two possible meanings of this phrase, which may indicate either (1) "a helper corresponding to him, a helper as in front of him"; or (2) "a helper against him": "Man and woman represent two opposites, who, if man is worthy merge into a unified whole . . . but when they are not worthy the very fact that they are opposites causes her to be 'against him.'"[4] The wife is neither man's shadow nor a servant. Rather, she helps as his other self in a dimension beyond any other creature. The woman is a helper as his life companion and soulmate.[5] From a Protestant perspective,

4. Zlotowitz and Scherman, Bereishis (ספר בראשית) Genesis, 1:104.
5. Cassuto, Commentary on Genesis: Part I, 128.

Keil writes that the woman not only helped the man "to perpetuate and multiply his race," but also to "fulfil his calling . . . to cultivate and govern the earth."[6] At the turn of the modern critical period, S. R. Driver concluded this helper was to assist the man, and at the same time provide companionship with an interchange of thought as intellectual equals.[7] More recently, Gordon J. Wenham concludes that "helper" does not imply the helper is stronger than the one helped, but rather that the latter's strength is inadequate on its own. Moreover, Wenham follows Delitzsch, who understood the phrase "matching him, corresponding to him" (כנגדו, *kenegdo*) to express complementarity rather than identity since the more natural phrase would have been כמוהו (*kamohu*, "like him") if identity were meant.[8]

Genesis 2:18	
MT	וַיֹּאמֶר יְהוָה אֱלֹהִים לֹא־טוֹב הֱיוֹת הָאָדָם לְבַדּוֹ אֶעֱשֶׂה־לּוֹ עֵזֶר כְּנֶגְדּוֹ:
LXX	καὶ εἶπεν κύριος ὁ θεός οὐ καλὸν εἶναι τὸν ἄνθρωπον μόνον ποιήσωμεν αὐτῷ βοηθὸν κατ' αὐτόν
Tg.	וַאֲמַר יוי אֱלֹהִים לָא תָקֵין טב דְיהֵי אָדָם בִלְחוֹדוֹהִי אַעֲבֵיד לֵיה סְמָד בְּקַבְלֵיה:
Vg.	*dixit quoque Dominus Deus non est bonum esse hominem solum faciamus ei adiutorium similem sui*
ESV	Then the LORD God said, "It is not good that the man should be alone; I will make him a helper fit for him."
NET	The LORD God said, "It is not good for the man to be alone. I will make a companion for him who corresponds to him."
NASB	Then the LORD God said, "It is not good for the man to be alone; I will make him a helper suitable for him."
NKJV	And the LORD God said, "*It is* not good that man should be alone; I will make him a helper comparable to him."
NIV	The LORD God said, "It is not good for the man to be alone. I will make a helper suitable for him."
NLT	Then the LORD God said, "It is not good for the man to be alone. I will make a helper who is just right for him."

Table 2.4. The text and translations of Genesis 2:18

6. Keil and Delitzsch, *Commentary on the Old Testament*, 1:54.

7. Driver, *Book of Genesis*, 41.

8. Wenham, *Genesis 1–15*, 68.

However, in looking not only to the ancient understanding of these words but also to their usage elsewhere within the Old Testament, what do the words עֵזֶר (*ezer*, "help, helper") and כְּנֶגְדּוֹ (*kenegdo*, "corresponding to, suitable for") mean and how are they used? The word עֵזֶר (*ezer*) is used some twenty-one times within the Old Testament as a noun. Quite often it is used to refer to God helping humanity (seventeen of twenty-one occurrences), as in Psalm 70:6, where the Lord is praised as a help and deliverer in reference to working salvation.[9] Elsewhere, it is used as in Genesis 2:18, 20 in reference to human help or aid. In Isaiah 30:5 the Lord declares that Egypt brings Israel neither help nor profit, and in Ezekiel 12:14 the Lord declares in judgment against the leaders of Jerusalem that he will scatter the prince's helpers and troops. Although those who argue for the egalitarian viewpoint claim that since God helps man this word cannot refer to hierarchical status, one is on firmer analytical ground considering agency as a component of semantic value. Accordingly, an accurate and detailed semantic analysis will distinguish between divine and human agency for עֵזֶר (*ezer*). Although both divine and human agents will share the same basic semantic value, divine agency merits a separate sense or usage classification. In Ezekiel 12:14 this word clearly refers to officials who are subordinate to the prince in Jerusalem. Therefore, it is safe to say that the semantic focus of this word is on the role and function of giving help or aid to someone across all sense and usage groups, and when this word is used in reference to a human agent, as distinct from divine agency, this may sometimes carry contextual implications of one who helps someone in a position of authority over them. However, this authority does not necessarily entail that of master to slave, nor does it refer to base servitude. Rather, it refers to help in the sense of ministry, encouragement, and loyalty.

Moreover, context suggests that usage of עֵזֶר (*ezer*, "help, helper") in Genesis 2:18, 20 is analogous to human agency in Ezekiel 12:14 rather than to contexts with divine agency. Foremost,

9. Exod 18:4; Deut 33:7, 26, 29; Ps 20:2; 33:20; 70:6; 89:19; 115:9, 10, 11; 121:1, 2; 124:8; 146:5; Dan 11:34; Hos 13:9.

the purpose of the narrative in Genesis 2:18–25 is stated explicitly in 2:18 as the quest for a helper for Adam. Adam named the animals, and naming within the Bible and the Ancient Near East indicated power or authority over the one named. Thus, Adam named the animals in Genesis 2:19 and possessed authority over them (Gen 1:26; Ps 8:6–8). However, among the animals there was found no helper suitable for him (Gen 2:20). This in turn led to the creation of woman (Gen 2:22–23), of whom Adam states, "This at last is bone of my bones and flesh of my flesh; she shall be called Woman, because she was taken out of Man" (Gen 2:23). This act of naming suggests that Adam, who is the prototype for all men, possessed authority in some manner over the woman. Therefore, woman is the source of help for man, who was in authority over her from creation.

In terms of reception history, this interpretation of Eve as Adam's helper is evidenced in deuterocanonical literature. The wedding prayer in Tobit 8:6 refers to God making Adam and giving Eve as his wife, helper, and support.

Tobit 8:6	
LXX	σὺ ἐποίησας Αδαμ καὶ ἔδωκας αὐτῷ βοηθὸν Ευαν στήριγμα τὴν γυναῖκα αὐτοῦ ἐκ τούτων ἐγενήθη τὸ ἀνθρώπων σπέρμα σὺ εἶπας οὐ καλὸν εἶναι τὸν ἄνθρωπον μόνον ποιήσωμεν αὐτῷ βοηθὸν ὅμοιον αὐτῷ
Vg.	*tu fecisti Adam de limo terrae dedistique ei adiutorium Evam*
NRSV	You made Adam, and for him you made his wife Eve as a helper and support. From the two of them the human race has sprung. You said, 'It is not good that the man should be alone; let us make a helper for him like himself.'

Table 2.5. The text and translations of Tobit 8:6

Thus, the Jewish community receiving the tradition of Genesis 2 understood it to mean woman was created in order to help and support man. In turning to patristic literature, Clement of Alexandria understood the word "helper" to refer to a woman's role in bearing and caring for children.[10] The manner in which Tertullian quotes Genesis 2:18 suggests he viewed companionship as the chief blessing of the helpmate: "The self-same Goodness provided also a help meet for him, that there might be nothing in his lot that was not good. For, said He, that the man be alone is not good."[11] Methodius expounds his allegorical interpretation of the church as Christ's helpmate, and describes the manner in which the church nurtures its children for Christ.[12] Similarly, St. Augustine evidences an understanding of *adiutorium* ("help") and *adiutor* ("helper") in Genesis 2 in reference to bearing children in order to obey the command to be fruitful and multiply.[13] Ambrose likewise understood that the woman was given to man both for companionship and for bearing children.[14] Therefore, during the intertestamental period the Jewish wedding rite indicates that woman was created as the helper of man. Later, the church fathers understood woman to help man by providing companionship, bearing children, and caring for them.

Excursus: Walter Kaiser and "Helpmate"

Walter Kaiser challenges the traditional understanding of עֵזֶר (*ezer*, "helper") based upon a rather convoluted argument.[15] Kaiser argues instead that this word means "power, authority" because two separate Hebrew phonemes coalesced so the initial letter of two separate words for "help, helper" and "power, authority" were confused. As warrant for his argument, Kaiser follows Bushnell's proposal that the traditional translation of ἐξουσίαν (*exousian*) in 1 Corinthians 11:10 is based on the

10. Clement, *Stromata* 2.23 (*ANF* 2:377–78).

11. Tertullian, *Five Books against Marcion* 2.4 (*ANF* 3:300). Cf. Chrysostom, *Homilies on Paul's Epistles to the Romans*, Homily 23 (*NPNF* 1.11, n.p.); Gregory of Nazianzus, "On the Death of His Father" (*NPNF* 2.7:256).

12. Methodius, *Banquet of the Ten Virgins* 8 (*ANF* 6:320).

13. Augustine, *On Genesis*, 376–80.

14. Ambrose, *Dogmatic Treatises, Ethical Works, and Sermons* (*NPNF* 2.10:23).

15. Kaiser, "Paul, Women and the Church"; Kaiser, "Correcting Caricatures."

gnostic Valentinus' confusion of homonyms in Coptic. Valentinus supposedly confused *ouershishi* ("power, authority") for *ouershoun* ("veil") around AD 140. This confusion, in turn, led to mistranslations by Clement and Origen, which to this day influence the mistranslation of 1 Corinthians 11:10 as "veil, symbol of authority" rather than "power." On the basis of Paul's supposed teaching that women are to have "power" on or upon their head equal to a man in 1 Corinthians 11:10, Kaiser argues that עֵזֶר (*ezer*, "help[er]") in Gen 2:18, 20 means "power, authority" rather than "help(er)." However, the LXX rendering βοηθὸν (*boēthon*, "helper") in Genesis 2:18, 20 dates to around 250 BC, which precedes Paul by at least 250 years and Valentinus by 390 years. Moreover, the Genesis Targum (dating between the first and fourth centuries AD) agrees with the Septuagint, was not influenced by Clement and Origen, and renders this word סְמָךְ (*semakh*, "helper"). Furthermore, intertestamental literature evidences the meaning βοηθὸν (*boēthon*, "helper") in the traditional Jewish wedding vow recorded in Tobit 8:6. Thus, the traditional rendering "helper," rather than Kaiser's proposed "power, authority," aligns more closely with earlier translation equivalents, in addition to clear evidence from reception history. Therefore, alongside his appeal to later Hebrew usage, Kaiser's argument seems to place one doubtful speculation upon another, introduces semantic anachronism into his historical-linguistic analysis, and builds his argument upon a phonological coalescence that occurred sometime during the second millennium BC. Historical linguistic analysis proves more reliable for demonstrating grammatical and phonological processes through time, whereas semantic values shift with fluidity. Thus, Kaiser seems to espouse "the conduit metaphor" of meaning in proposing that Paul was aware of a second millennium BC meaning during the first century AD of which the Septuagint translators (250 BC) and the authors of the intertestamental literature before him were ignorant.[16]

16. The conduit metaphor of meaning may be associated with some

In turning to the next constituent of the phrase "a helper suitable for him," what is the meaning of the phrase כְּנֶגְדּוֹ (kenegdo, "corresponding to, suitable for")? The particle כְּ (ke) is a preposition indicating similarity or likeness and is normally glossed "like, as."[17] The preposition נֶגֶד (neged) means "that which is opposite, that which corresponds." As noted by Koehler-Baumgartner, the use of this preposition in Genesis 2:18, 20 indicates the meaning "like his opposite, proper for him."[18] One should note, however, that this construction is a compound preposition, and complex prepositions in Hebrew may either result in a meaning that is not a sum of their parts, or the compounding may represent more accurately the relation in question.[19] This rather general definition of compound prepositions does not prove helpful, and so we therefore look to early translations in order to approximate the earliest attested meaning of the construction. The received understanding of early translations suggests that this compounding follows the basic trajectory of the meaning of the component prepositions in order to represent more accurately the relationship between the man and the woman. Around 250 BC, the translators of the Septuagint rendered the Hebrew phrase βοηθὸν κατ᾽ αὐτόν (boēthon kat' auton, "a helper corresponding/in conformity with him"). This understanding was in turn taken up by the Vulgate (fourth century AD), *faciamus ei adiutorium simile sui* ("let us make for him help/assistance similar to him"). *Targum Onqelos*, which is an Aramaic translation providing a window into the received Jewish understanding of these words during the early centuries of the church, renders this phrase אֲעֲבֵיד לֵיה סְמָךְ כְּקִבְלֵיה (ʾaʿabed leh semakh keqivleh, "I shall make for him a support/help corresponding to/alongside of/opposite him"). Moreover, this prepositional construction suggests complementarity, and the use of the compound

dubious practitioners of historical linguistics or cognate analysis, who assume a stable semantic value through long periods of time or across language families, akin to water flowing through a conduit.

17. GKC §§102c, 118s–x; Joüon §133g; IBHS 11.2.9.

18. HALOT 1:666.

19. IBHS 11.3a, 11.3.3.

preposition brings focus on the nature of this relationship. Thus, the Lord God created woman as a helpmate "corresponding to, proper for" the man. As noted above, Gordon Wenham follows Franz Delitzsch in observing that this phrase does not indicate similar identity with sameness between male and female. Rather, this phrase indicates complementarity with mutual support.[20]

As this narrative continues, Adam declares, "This is now bone of my bones, and flesh of my flesh; she shall be called Woman, because she was taken out of Man" (Gen 2:23). With this statement, the man indicates the nature of the relationship between the two. The quest for a helper "according to his likeness" (כְּנֶגְדּוֹ, *kenegdo*) from 2:18, 20 has now been achieved with the creation of woman. She is "bone of my bones, and flesh of my flesh." In other words, the man now has a helper who is similar to him, and they share corresponding needs and gifts. This general characteristic of the relationship between men and women is the foundation for complementarity in marriage. The created similarities provide the framework within which the complementary differences between male and female complete the Creator's intentions so that the man leaves his father and mother in order to be joined into one flesh with his wife (Gen 2:24).

However, this complementarity is disrupted in Genesis 3. As is well known, the serpent enters into dialogue with the woman and contradicts the command not to eat from the tree which is in the middle of the garden by stating, "You surely will not die! For God knows that in the day you eat from it your eyes will be opened, and you will be like God, knowing good and evil" (Gen 3:4–5). As a result, the woman saw that the tree was good for food and desirable to make one wise. In direct contradiction of the Lord God's earlier command that Adam not eat from the tree of the knowledge of good and evil (Gen 2:15–17), the woman took from its fruit, ate, gave also to her husband, and he ate (Gen 3:6). Therefore, with this act the woman no longer fulfilled her created

20. Keil and Delitzsch, *Commentary on the Old Testament*; Gunkel, *Genesis*, 11; Driver, *Book of Genesis*, 41–42; Rad, *Genesis*, 82; Westermann, *Genesis 1–11*, 227; Wenham, *Genesis 1–15*, 68.

duty of helping her husband obey the Lord God in the garden. Rather, she initiated disobedience to the Lord God's command. This narrative subtly suggests that the woman's role was to help her husband obey the Lord's commands and complement him in caring for the garden in which they were placed. However, she listened to the serpent rather than to the command given to her husband and she chose to disobey the Lord God. Moreover, the man took the fruit unquestioningly and followed her in eating from the tree of the knowledge of good and evil. Thus, he lacked initiative and failed to safeguard their obedience to the Lord's command. Furthermore, where was the man when the serpent approached the woman and entered into dialogue? Assuming a close relationship (Gen 2:24–25), the man should have been aware of his wife's temptation and intervened to help her. His passive neglect, in turn, led to his own downfall. This narrative characterizes the tendency of fallen men, who ignore the spiritual state of their wife, and who passively allow her to succumb to temptation. They fail to protect her through prayer and careful obedience to the commands of God by maintaining close relationship with her, as well as godliness within the marriage.

After the man blamed the woman, and after the woman blamed the serpent (Gen 3:8–13), the Lord God passed judgment on all three (Gen 3:14–19). It is at this point that the woman received the judgment of increased pain in childbirth, and the Lord God declared that she will long for her husband, who will rule over her (Gen 3:16). Although he previously possessed authority over the woman and she was to be his helpmate, the fall marred this relationship. The Lord God declared that the woman will long for her husband, who will now rule over her. The word for "rule" (מָשַׁל, *mashal*) connotes an authority of mastery or dominion over the one being ruled. Therefore, the authority of man over woman did not begin with the fall. Rather, it increased in intensity and pain, analogous to the woman's increased pain in childbirth. The Lord God then passed judgment over the man, who remained passive throughout this entire narrative. The man ate from the tree which God commanded that he should not eat rather than protecting Eve and leading her out of temptation (Gen 3:17–19). Accordingly, his toil increased and they were both banished from the garden lest they also eat from the tree of life (Gen 3:22–24).

In sum, it is noteworthy that Adam's act of naming precedes the fall, and it follows the depiction of woman being fashioned from the rib next to Adam's heart. This suggests that the loving authority of man over woman was an act of creation, in contrast to the fallen domination of man over woman. John Calvin put it well when commenting on Genesis 2:18–25:

> . . . the voice of God is rather to be heard, which declares that woman is given as a companion and an associate to the man, to assist him to live well. I confess, indeed, that in this corrupt state of mankind, the blessing of God, which is here described, is neither perceived nor flourishes; but the cause of the evil must be considered, namely, that the order of nature, which God had appointed, has been inverted by us. For if the integrity of man had remained to this day such as it was from the beginning, that divine institution would be clearly discerned, and the sweetest harmony would reign in marriage; because the husband would look up with reverence to God; the woman in this would be a faithful assistant to him; and both, with one consent, would cultivate a holy, as well as friendly and peaceful intercourse. Now, it has happened by our fault, and by the corruption of nature, that this happiness of marriage has, in a great measure, perished, or, at least, is mixed and infected with many inconveniences. Hence arise strifes, troubles, sorrows, dissensions, and a boundless sea of evils; and hence it follows, that men are often disturbed by their wives, and suffer through them many discouragements. Still, marriage was not capable of being so far vitiated by the depravity of men, that the blessing which God has once sanctioned by his word should be utterly abolished and extinguished. Therefore, amidst many inconveniences of marriage, which are the fruits of degenerate nature, some residue of divine good remains; as in the fire apparently smothered, some sparks still glitter. On this main point hangs another, that women, being instructed in their duty of helping their husbands,

should study to keep this divinely appointed order. It is also the part of men to consider what they owe in return to the other half of their kind, for the obligation of both sexes is mutual, and on this condition is the woman assigned as a help to the man, that he may fill the place of her head and leader.[21]

Therefore, from this reading of Genesis 2:4—3:24, one may conclude that the created role of man is to care for the garden in which he was placed. Adam's role included the primary initiative in relationship, and the role of woman was to help the man. However, with the fall the nature of this relationship devolved from authority to domination. The woman experienced increased pain both in labor and marriage. Thus, it is not the case that male authority is a result of the fall. Rather, the fall distorted male authority. Therefore, it is not the goal of redemption history to reverse the fall by completely removing woman from the authority of man. In fact, removing male authority participates in the fall when Eve leads Adam. Rather, redemption aims to reverse the distorted elements of male authority, as well as the distorted elements of created feminine purpose, such as abuse and demeaning servitude. The quest to define these elements merits a consideration of select narratives from the Pentateuch, to which we next turn. These narratives illustrate the need for covenant in God's plan for redeeming the elect.

3. Distorted Roles in Pentateuchal Narrative

Although many narratives may apply, we shall narrow discussion to the texts of Genesis 12, 16, and Numbers 12 in order to illustrate the manner in which the roles of men and women were distorted with the fall and in need of restoration through the covenant. In many other narratives men clearly lead in transgression, yet these have been chosen on account of the manner in which they echo the fall in Genesis 3.

---

21. Calvin, *Genesis*, 129–30.

One may identify an initial account of fallen male headship in Abram's sojourn into Egypt in Genesis 12:10–20. There was a famine in the land, so Abram went down to Egypt. As they drew near, Abram told Sarai that because she was a beautiful woman the Egyptians would kill him if she were identified as his wife (Gen 12:11–12). Therefore, Abram asked her to tell the Egyptians that she was his sister that he may live (Gen 12:13). The Egyptians saw Sarai was beautiful, they commended her to Pharaoh, she was taken to Pharaoh's house, and Abram received sheep, oxen, male donkeys, male and female servants, female donkeys, and camels (Gen 12:14–16). However, the Lord plagued Pharaoh and his house on account of Sarai, therefore Pharaoh confronted Abram over the deception, and sent him away with his wife and possessions (Gen 12:17–20).

When read as preparation for the Mosaic covenant, Abram and Sarai's troubles begin with Abram's decision to bear false witness in Egypt (contra Exod 20:16). The first calling of men under the covenant is to obey covenant ethics. Moreover, although Sarai is "bone of his bone and flesh of his flesh," Abram fails to trust the Lord's protection by declaring Sarai as his wife in order to protect her both from harm and defilement. Instead, the narrative presents Abram as concerned about his own safety with little or no concern for the safety of his wife. Not only did Abram trade the integrity of his family and the purity of his wife in order to save his own skin, but he also took wealth from Pharaoh for her. Thus, Abram typifies fallen men who value their life more than their wife, as well as men who sacrifice their marriage for wealth and possessions.

Second, within Genesis 16:1–16, Sarai had borne Abram no children. According to the custom of the time, Sarai offered her female Egyptian servant Hagar to Abram in order to have children by her. Hagar was given as Abram's wife after they lived ten years in the land of Canaan (Gen 16:3). Rather than preserving the created marriage ideal of one man and one woman (Gen 1:26–28; 2:4–25), Sarai embraced the local customs, sought a second wife for her husband, and Abram followed the practice. Thus, Sarai sought to fulfill the Lord's promise of a son by alternate means (Gen 15:4), and "Abram listened to the voice of Sarai" rather than remaining loyal to one wife (Gen 16:2). This second wife led to turmoil within the patriarchal family when Hagar looked with contempt on her mistress, was cast out, and then the angel of the Lord commanded her to return to Sarai and submit herself to her mistress (Gen 16:4–16).[22]

Therefore, the subtle understatement of this narrative suggests the parallel between Adam and Abram's passive behavior, as well as Eve and Sarai taking the initiative and leading their husbands contrary to the Lord's revealed will. In this case, Sarai led her husband to transgress the ideal of one husband and one wife established by the Lord at creation. The Hagar narrative develops this theme by suggesting that those within the covenant should not resort to human means in helping the Lord fulfill his own promises. Moreover, it is not permissible to supplant or mix the covenant ideal of marriage with conflicting local customs. The elect are to remain pure, and women are to guard their marriages as the foundation for the Lord's blessings and promises. Women are called to know the Lord's covenant ideals and to influence their husband accordingly rather than leading their husband astray. Moreover, husbands are called to practice discernment rather than acquiescing to violations of the covenant like both Adam and Abram.

Third, in Numbers 12:1–16 Miriam and Aaron spoke against Moses because of his Cushite wife. The Lord called the three of them to the tent of meeting, and then from a pillar of cloud called Aaron and Miriam forward. The Lord declared that with most prophets he made himself known by vision or dream, yet he spoke clearly by mouth with Moses. The Lord's anger was kindled, and when the cloud departed Miriam was leprous like snow. Moses prayed on her behalf, and the Lord commanded that she be put outside the camp for seven days due to uncleanness. The narrative provides at least two indications that Miriam instigated this incident. First, it begins with Miriam's name preceding Aaron's in 12:1, whereas women tend not to appear as subjects in classical Hebrew narrative unless they play a major part in its development.

---

22. This turmoil parallels that which follows Jacob marrying multiple wives in Gen 28–50.

Not only is Miriam mentioned, but her name precedes that of her brother, the high priest. Second, the Lord's judgment falls fully on Miriam rather than Aaron. This suggests that the Lord judged the one who was the driving force behind the challenge to Moses' authority.

Therefore, Miriam's actions echo and develop the theme of Eve leading Adam in several ways (Gen 3:1–9). Foremost, this narrative suggests that notable women are to use their influence with men like Aaron in order to foster respect for the Lord's chosen prophets and leaders, and in order to quell disruptions to communal unity. Second, this narrative suggests that women do indeed have a voice and influence within their created role. Accordingly, they bear the responsibility of moderating urges to challenge the authority of leaders chosen by God. Third, men like Aaron are called to practice discernment and restraint by curtailing rather than passively following challenges to godly leadership. Contrary to the rhetoric often employed by Christian feminists, the complementarian view does not call women to submit blindly to abusive relationships. Rather, women are called to submit themselves to the servant leadership established by God from creation and revealed through the covenants. Similarly, men are called to actively protect unity in recognition of the divine authority given to the leader chosen by the Lord.

From the created roles of men and women and the distortion of these roles with the fall, we now turn to two key passages regarding the roles of men and women in the Historical Books (Joshua through 2 Chronicles).

Chapter 3

Man and Woman in the Historical Books

WE NOW TURN TO two narratives from the Historical Books (Joshua–2 Chronicles), which are often mentioned in support of the argument that the Bible teaches women may lead: the judge Deborah (Judg 4–5) and Huldah the prophetess (2 Kgs 22).[1] Since Deborah led Israel, and since Huldah was consulted regarding the legitimacy of the Torah scroll found in the temple, it is argued that Israel's history provides evidence that passages such as 2 Timothy 2:12–15 have been illegitimately universalized and retrojected back on the history of Israel when women actually enjoyed much more freedom than during the so-called dark ages of patriarchal

1. Critical scholars refer to the unit of Joshua–2 Kings as the Deuteronomistic History. The account of the Deuteronomistic History put forth by Martin Noth and espoused by many critical biblical scholars hypothesizes that legal portions of Deuteronomy are older traditions, to which were added introductory and concluding materials around the time of the exile. The traditions within Joshua through 2 Kings were then edited by a circle of Deuteronomistic editors. The Cartesian and deistic assumptions behind this critical approach stand in stark contrast to the present reading, which assumes divine revelation, inspiration, and the historical validity of Christian Scripture. The present writer regards the entire book of Deuteronomy as an authentic, Mosaic composition, reliably presented, dating to Moses' lifetime, and finalized under Joshua no later than the generation following Moses' death. The Deuteronomistic books were then compiled and edited under the influence of the book of Deuteronomy from the time of Joshua, through the periods of the judges and kings, and into the exile.

dominance. Consequently, it is argued, women may lead and teach within the church. However, in order to evaluate these two historical accounts in relation to the roles of men and women, we must first establish basic principles for interpreting the historical books in the light of their literary structure and function.

1. Principles for Reading the Historical Books Accurately

Although one occasionally encounters an interpretation of a discrete narrative from Joshua through 2 Kings which uses these materials as a foundation for ethical teaching, most sound interpreters regard these books either as an illustration of obeying the Torah (Genesis through Deuteronomy), or as an illustration of the consequences for violating it. In other words, whereas the legal portions of the Five Books of Moses are normative for understanding the covenant and ethics, the Historical Books interpret Israel's history prophetically on the foundation of the Law as a warning to future generations. Moreover, this style of writing continues this principle from the narrative portions of the Pentateuch, where narrative portions illustrate the need for covenant law through the shortcomings of the antediluvians and patriarchs. As one example of a non-normative text, the description of King Solomon in 1 Kings 10:14–11:8 does not legitimate the acquiring of wealth by authoritarian regimes today. Rather, this unit is intended to be read in the light of Deuteronomy 17:14–20 as practice for the ideal reader to learn how to apply the Law in order to discern between right and wrong. Thus, whereas the ethical commands of the Torah are normative and foundational, the Historical Books facilitate the application of the Law to the history of Israel in order to enable subsequent generations to develop discernment in applying it to their own time. Therefore, there will be some positive characters, some negative, and many who fall somewhere between the two ends of the continuum. It remains for the reader to wrestle with each episode and with each character in order to determine the exact relationship between a given narrative and the ethical standards of the Mosaic covenant.

A second principle of interpretation includes the notion that an individual narrative unit, such as the Samson narrative (Judg 13–16), is to be read in the light of the entire book. The failings of Samson are one means of characterizing the failings of Israel before there was a king. The echoic phrase "In those days there was no king in Israel; everyone did what was right in his own eyes" (Judg 17:6; 18:1; 19:1; 21:25) indicates the purpose of the book and retrospectively colors the interpretation of the individual narrative units leading up to them. Each of the stories in the book of Judges, including the Samson narrative, illustrates the downward spiral of the people as they moved farther from the Mosaic ideal of loyalty to the covenant. Therefore, reading each of these units as if they were prescriptions for the godly ideal of holiness misses the point of the narrative, akin to reading the dialogues of Job's friends as if they were prescriptive for comforting someone in affliction. In each of these cases, the narrative framework provides the proper context for rightly understanding the contents of the book. Thus, the narrative of Deborah in Judges 4–5 is to be read in the light of the evaluative statements which inform the literary framework of the book of Judges. Likewise, the narrative of Huldah the prophetess (2 Kgs 22:8–20; 2 Chron 34:14–28) is to be read in the light of the impending downfall of Jerusalem and Judah, which is both the climactic and didactic point of Kings and Chronicles.[2] Historical narrative uses the real-life foibles of figures and institutions in order to lead the ideal reader to correct similar tendencies in their own life.

2. Deborah as a Leader in Judges 4–5

When discussing the issue of women in positions of leadership and teaching within the church, egalitarians often cite the judge

2. For example, I would argue that Bilezikian (*Beyond Sex Roles*, 52–53) reads the discrete narratives of Deborah and Huldah as prescriptive and misses their didactic point situated within literary context. Literary context leads the reader to wrestle with their roles in the light of Israel's ethical devolution, and this viewed in terms of the primacy of Torah in Genesis through Deuteronomy. This also holds true for Belleville, "Women Leaders in the Bible"; Brown, "What About Deborah?"; and Pierce, "Deborah."

Deborah as an example from Israel's history legitimating women serving as leaders today. This, therefore, merits a consideration of the narrative of Deborah situated within its literary context in the book of Judges.

The cycle of faithfulness-idolatry-judgment-repentance-deliverance is one of the better-known literary features of the book of Judges. Early in this series of cycles, Israel did what was evil in the sight of the Lord following the death of the judge Ehud. Accordingly, the Lord allowed Israel to be oppressed severely by Jabin, a Canaanite king, for twenty years (Judg 4:1–3). At this time, Deborah, both a prophetess and the wife of Lappidoth, judged Israel between Bethel and Ramah (Judg 4:4–5). The Lord spoke to her and commanded that Barak march to Mount Tabor with ten thousand men of Naphtali and Zebulun so that the Lord might hand Sisera, the commander of Jabin's army, into Barak's hand at the river Kishon (Judg 4:6–7). Barak responded, "If you will go with me, then I will go; but if you will not go with me, I will not go" (Judg 4:8) Deborah acquiesced, but warned that the honor of victory would not be his. Rather, Sisera would be given into the hands of a woman (Judg 4:9). Deborah went with Barak to Kedesh and the Lord routed the army of Sisera so that none were left (Judg 4:12–16). Sisera fled on foot to the tent of Jael, the wife of Heber the Kenite, who entreated him to enter her tent for hiding. He fell sound asleep after drinking the milk she gave him, and so Jael drove a tent peg into his temple, killing him. As Barak pursued Sisera, Jael met Barak and took him to Sisera's body. Thus, God subdued Jabin the king of Canaan (Judg 4:12–24).

At first glance, this story seems to legitimate the leadership of a woman in ancient Israel. Not only was she a recognized judge to whom the sons of Israel came for judgment, but the Lord also spoke through her.[3] It stands to reason that if the Lord spoke to her, then her leadership must have been approved by him.

---

3. The role of Deborah as a prophetess is not in question since prophetesses were legitimate under the Mosaic covenant (Exod 15:20–21). This likewise holds true for Huldah in the following discussion.

However, as with the dialogues of Job, literary context proves crucial to a right reading. Within the story itself, Deborah first urged Barak to march on Sisera alone (Judg 4:6). Moreover, after agreeing to go with Barak, Deborah informed him that the Lord would in turn give Sisera into the hands of a woman rather than into his hands (Judg 4:9). This narrative description indicates that since Barak was unwilling to trust the Lord alone, and since Barak insisted that Deborah go with him, the Lord brought victory in a manner shameful to Barak. Furthermore, that the Lord spoke to Deborah does not necessarily indicate that a prophetess as judge accorded with the Lord's ideal. For example, in Numbers 22–24 the Lord spoke to the idolatrous prophet Balaam multiple times, both through his donkey and directly, and yet Balaam's death in Israel's revenge on Midian indicates the Lord's disapproval (Num 31:8). In this case, Deborah herself notes the shamefulness of a man not leading Israel's troops into battle. Deborah urged Barak to lead, and yet Barak abdicated his leadership role.

Moreover, as was mentioned above in relation to the Samson narrative, the entire book of Judges is structured in order to demonstrate both the spiritual and the political devolution of Israel from the death of Joshua (Judg 1:1) to the point where each man did what was right in his own eyes because there was no king in the land (Judg 21:25). The repetition and echo of the phrase "In those days there was no king in Israel; everyone did what was right in his own eyes" (Judg 17:6; 18:1; 19:1; 21:25) emphasizes this point in the final chapters of the book. Accordingly, everything which precedes these statements in the book of Judges is to be read as a gradual turning from the Mosaic ideal of a prophet like himself (Deut 18:15–22) to virtual anarchy, and each narrative unit is to be read with an eye toward divergences from the Mosaic Law and how these divergences contribute to spiritual decay. Thus, the narrative of Deborah and Barak in Judges 4–5 is one such step in this process.[4]

In particular, as was noted in the discussion of Genesis 1–3, the Law was prefaced with the creation narrative outlining the ideal order and the fallen order of male and female relationships. The

---

4. Bordwine, *Pauline Doctrine of Male Headship*, 287–88.

created purpose of the woman was to be a helpmate corresponding to her husband. However, here in Judges 4 we see Deborah judging Israel rather than devoting herself fully to helping her husband, Lappidoth. Moreover, that the Lord speaks to the nation through Deborah rather than through the priests or a prophet like unto Moses (Deut 18:15) indicates the low spiritual tide in the priestly establishment and among the people. Although the Law describes Moses' sister Miriam as a prophetess, she spoke to and led women rather than men (Exod 15:20–21).[5] Thus, the Deborah narrative implies disapproval of the passive and faithless men of that time. In particular, the unwillingness of Barak to trust the Lord fully and lead the attack against Sisera exemplifies the passivity associated with a lack of faith as well as echoing the passiveness of Adam in the garden (Gen 3). The promise of God alone was not enough for Barak. He wanted Deborah the prophetess to accompany him as further assurance. Each of these subtle points indicates the reason why Israel needs a king who will lead them back to the covenant ideal of Moses. Indeed, this ideal king will turn the nation from doing what is right in its own eyes, and will lead them to keep covenant with the Lord.

Therefore, as this discussion suggests, the leadership of Deborah within Israel was not an ethical ideal. Rather, it was an indication of the spiritual decay in Israel, and it was one of the initial steps toward the spiritual and political anarchy reached by the end of the book. Moreover, this narrative suggests that historical periods where men abdicate their leadership role within the covenant community lead to periods of anarchy and rebellion against the Lord.

3. Huldah the Prophetess in 2 Kings

Another exemplar often noted in support of females in the teaching role of the church is that of Huldah the prophetess (2 Kgs 22:8–20; 2 Chr 34:14–28). According to this account, the wicked

5. References to a "prophetess" are found in Exod 15:20; Judg 4:4; 2 Kgs 22:14; 2 Chr 34:22; Neh 6:14; Isa 8:3.

King Manasseh was succeeded by his son Josiah, who took care to ensure the repair of the temple (2 Kgs 22:1–7). During the course of the repairs, Hilkiah the high priest reported to Shaphan the scribe that he found the book of the Law. Shaphan read it and reported the find to the king, who also read it. In response, King Josiah tore his clothes and commanded his ministers to inquire of the Lord both for him and for the people of Judah on account of the wrath of God resulting from their disobedience to the book of the Law (2 Kgs 22:8–13). Accordingly, Hilkiah, Ahikam, Achbor, Shaphan, and Asaiah went to "Huldah the prophetess, the wife of Shallum" (2 Kgs 22:14). Thereupon, Huldah reported that due to the idolatry of the land the Lord would indeed bring evil according to the words of the Law. However, because Josiah humbled himself before the Lord he would see peace during his days, and the imminent judgment would be withheld until after Josiah's death (2 Kgs 22:15–20). During his lifetime, Josiah then renewed the covenant (2 Kgs 23:1–3), purified the land (2 Kgs 23:4–20), and reinstituted the Passover (2 Kgs 23:21–27). Following the wicked reigns of Jehoahaz, Jehoiakim, Jehoiachin, and Zedekiah (2 Kgs 23:28–24:20), the city of Jerusalem fell to the Babylonian king Nebuchadnezzar, and the temple was plundered and burned (2 Kgs 25:1–21).

As with the story of Deborah, the prophetess and judge, it is likewise possible upon a cursory reading to find support for female leadership and teaching in the story of Huldah the prophetess. However, upon further reflection the literary context of this narrative suggests otherwise. According to the interpretive principles outlined at the beginning of this section, the understated nature of historical narrative points out the spiritual deficiencies within Israel at various points in the nation's history. Like the story of Deborah, the story of Huldah makes this point. That there were no male prophets from whom the king's ministers could seek a word from the Lord emphasizes the spiritual drought in Judah and Jerusalem directly following the rule of Manasseh and Amon.[6] Thus, the place-

6. It is assumed that Jeremiah, the son of Hilkiah the priest, had not yet been influenced by the Law and arisen as a prophet during these early days of Josiah's reign.

ment of this account regarding Huldah at precisely this point in the historical narrative makes the opposite point from that for which it is often cited. This is not a historical event establishing the propriety of female teachers within the church. Quite the opposite. The appeal to Huldah the prophetess indicates the dire straits in which the Jerusalem religious establishment found itself. Jerusalem stood at such a distance from the Mosaic ideal that there were no more godly prophets whom the ministers could seek in order to authenticate the Law on the eve of Jerusalem's destruction.

Therefore, an examination of the accounts of Deborah and Huldah situated within their literary context leads to the conclusion that they are making a point opposite of that for which they are often cited. In direct relevance to the contemporary situation, they indicate that female leadership indicated a spiritual low tide in the history of Israel. These women filled a spiritual vacuum when no godly and vigorous men could be found. Thus, if a contextual reading of these passages informs our present outlook, we should humble ourselves before the Lord because the prevalence of women in positions of authority in various spiritual offices, and especially male deference to them, points toward our own spiritual drought and impending judgment. The appointment of women to positions of spiritual leadership over men is not something to be sought and glorified. Rather, it is indicative of the church's apostasy and the Lord's imminent wrath.[7]

---

7. For an account of how this is happening today, see Grudem, *Evangelical Feminism*. For one example of how the authority of the Bible is downplayed in feminist arguments, Ruth Tucker writes, "Stories show us the way. Indeed, stories, far more than biblical proof texting, show us how to work through the tough times of life. They also show us where both sides of the debate can meet on common ground" (*Black and White Bible*, 26). The contextual interpretation of the Bible has been downplayed as "proof-texting," and stories (that is, experience) are exalted above the objective truth of Scripture. Also at stake is the clarity of Scripture in the muddle of conflicting interpretations. When stories unify rather than Scripture, we have surely arrived in *haeresis*, "division." Might one suggest that a sympathetic and contextual reading of Scripture as delivered by apostolic tradition would lead both to unity and biblical integrity today rather than to the fragmentation of Christendom through conflicting stories?

Chapter 4

The Inspired and Authoritative New Testament Interpretation of the Old

WE NOW MOVE FROM the Old Testament to its reception in New Testament passages often cited regarding the roles of men and women. This is a basic presentation of the relevant passages, given a straightforward reading of the text in canonical context. Egalitarians and feminists reinterpret each point of the following discussion in support of their own position with detailed exegesis and argumentation. Nevertheless, the perspicuity of Scripture suggests that a straightforward reading of these texts is to be preferred over special hermeneutics (an atypical or dubious interpretive method not generally employed in other passages or reading in general), an unnecessarily complicated argument which confuses rather than clarifies, or an argument appealing to hypothetical historical background for which there is no unambiguous evidence extant.[1] These egalitarian arguments either have been answered or anticipated by the detailed grammatical, lexical, and historical

1. For an answer regarding the hypothetical historical setting to which egalitarians often appeal, see Baugh, "Foreign World." For an egalitarian's social-scientific critique of those who argue that Jesus founded an egalitarian sect, which later reverted to patriarchalism, see Elliott, "Jesus Was Not an Egalitarian."

analysis conducted by complementarian scholars such as those found in the edited volumes of Piper and Grudem (1991/2006) and Köstenberger and Schreiner (1995/2005). The present author finds these latter works to handle the evidence more faithfully and naturally than egalitarian writers, and recommends these works for further reading.[2] We shall consider 1 Corinthians 11:2–16; 14:33b–36; Galatians 3:28; 1 Timothy 2:12–15; and 1 Peter 3:1–7 in their canonical order. This discussion seeks first to demonstrate the manner in which Paul and Peter deliver their exegesis and application of Mosaic Torah, and second, to provide direct quotations and summaries of patristic interpretation as evidence for the initial reception of apostolic teaching regarding the created and redeemed roles of men and women.

1. Creation and Relationship Applied in 1 Corinthians 11:2–16

Several Pauline passages dealing with the ecclesiological roles of men and women refer to creation. Although Christian feminists argue that these were instructions for specific social situations within the early Christian community, the present investigation instead argues that Paul develops these discussions from his exegesis of the creation narratives in Genesis 1–3. Therefore, the Pauline instructions are not merely culturally conditioned reactions to a discrete situation within early Christian communities. Rather, they are exegetical appropriations of the creation and fall narratives for the universal church to apply in fledgling churches departing from scriptural practice. Their circulation within the early church provides further warrant for their universal authority.

---

2. Piper and Grudem, *Recovering Biblical Manhood and Womanhood*; Köstenberger and Schreiner, *Women in the Church*. Although egalitarian writers have published many treatments since 2006, the essays in Piper and Grudem, as well as in Köstenberger and Schreiner, follow the plain sense of the text more closely, and egalitarian critics have yet to provide a more felicitous reading.

The first passage we shall examine is 1 Corinthians 11:2–16, where Paul deals with the issue of the husband's headship over his wife.[3] Paul begins this unit by commending the Corinthians for maintaining the traditions he first received and then passed on to them (v. 2). This mention of traditions at the outset of the discussion is interesting in that Paul is not developing this discussion with a new application specific to the Corinthian situation alone. Rather, he casts the discussion in terms of the general scriptural tradition he received, which he then passed along specifically to the Corinthians. Therefore, the Corinthians are maintaining traditions which were not developed by Paul for their discrete situation; rather, they were delivered from the elders in the wider community to the believers in Corinth. As will be noted below, this discussion of "traditions" refers to Genesis 1:26–28; 2:18, 20; 2:21–22.

---

3. The present discussion is not intended to be an exhaustive exegesis of 1 Cor 11:2–16. Rather, the focus is upon Paul's use and understanding of Gen 1–3. For a more detailed exegetical discussion, see Schreiner, "Head Coverings, Prophecies, and the Trinity"; Bordwine, "1 Corinthians 11:3" and "1 Corinthians 11:4–16," in *Pauline Doctrine of Male Headship*, 15–80. Cf. Fee, "Praying and Prophesying in the Assemblies"; Peppiatt, *Women and Worship at Corinth*. Against such standard lexical works as *BDAG* (*kephalē*, "[2] a being of high status, *head*; [2a] in the case of living beings, to denote superior rank" in reference to the husband in 1 Cor 11:3b and Eph 5:23a, and in reference to Christ in Eph 1:22; 4:15; and 5:23b), egalitarians look to extrabiblical, classical usage in order to redefine "head, headship" as "source, origin," after excluding relevant NT evidence alongside writings directly following the NT period (Mickelsen and Mickelsen, "Does Male Dominance Tarnish Our Translations?"; Mickelsen and Mickelsen, "'Head' of the Epistles"). The study of Wayne Grudem ("Does *Kephalē* ['Head'] Mean 'Source' or 'Authority Over'?") provides a sound linguistic basis for understanding this word. Although egalitarians critique Grudem's analysis (e.g. Cervin, "Does *Kephalē* Mean 'Source' or 'Authority'?"; "On the Significance of *Kephalē* ["Head"]"), Grudem answers his critics and establishes the contextual meaning of this word in "Meaning of *Kephalē* ['Head']"). Also see Bordwine, *Pauline Doctrine of Headship*, 208–41. For the practical application of these principles, see Hall and Schemm, "Marriage as It Was Meant to Be Seen"; cf. Gabrielle, "Kephale as Fountainhead in 1 Corinthians 11:3."

1 Corinthians 11:2–16
² Ἐπαινῶ δὲ ὑμᾶς ὅτι πάντα μου μέμνησθε καί, καθὼς παρέδωκα ὑμῖν, τὰς παραδόσεις κατέχετε. ³ Θέλω δὲ ὑμᾶς εἰδέναι ὅτι παντὸς ἀνδρὸς ἡ κεφαλὴ ὁ Χριστός ἐστιν, κεφαλὴ δὲ γυναικὸς ὁ ἀνήρ, κεφαλὴ δὲ τοῦ Χριστοῦ ὁ θεός. ⁴ πᾶς ἀνὴρ προσευχόμενος ἢ προφητεύων κατὰ κεφαλῆς ἔχων καταισχύνει τὴν κεφαλὴν αὐτοῦ. ⁵ πᾶσα δὲ γυνὴ προσευχομένη ἢ προφητεύουσα ἀκατακαλύπτῳ τῇ κεφαλῇ καταισχύνει τὴν κεφαλὴν αὐτῆς· ἓν γάρ ἐστιν καὶ τὸ αὐτὸ τῇ ἐξυρημένῃ. ⁶ εἰ γὰρ οὐ κατακαλύπτεται γυνή, καὶ κειράσθω· εἰ δὲ αἰσχρὸν γυναικὶ τὸ κείρασθαι ἢ ξυρᾶσθαι, κατακαλυπτέσθω. ⁷ Ἀνὴρ μὲν γὰρ οὐκ ὀφείλει κατακαλύπτεσθαι τὴν κεφαλὴν εἰκὼν καὶ δόξα θεοῦ ὑπάρχων· ἡ γυνὴ δὲ δόξα ἀνδρός ἐστιν. ⁸ οὐ γάρ ἐστιν ἀνὴρ ἐκ γυναικὸς ἀλλὰ γυνὴ ἐξ ἀνδρός· ⁹ καὶ γὰρ οὐκ ἐκτίσθη ἀνὴρ διὰ τὴν γυναῖκα ἀλλὰ γυνὴ διὰ τὸν ἄνδρα. ¹⁰ διὰ τοῦτο ὀφείλει ἡ γυνὴ ἐξουσίαν ἔχειν ἐπὶ τῆς κεφαλῆς διὰ τοὺς ἀγγέλους. ¹¹ πλὴν οὔτε γυνὴ χωρὶς ἀνδρὸς οὔτε ἀνὴρ χωρὶς γυναικὸς ἐν κυρίῳ· ¹² ὥσπερ γὰρ ἡ γυνὴ ἐκ τοῦ ἀνδρός, οὕτως καὶ ὁ ἀνὴρ διὰ τῆς γυναικός· τὰ δὲ πάντα ἐκ τοῦ θεοῦ. ¹³ Ἐν ὑμῖν αὐτοῖς κρίνατε· πρέπον ἐστὶν γυναῖκα ἀκατακάλυπτον τῷ θεῷ προσεύχεσθαι; ¹⁴ οὐδὲ ἡ φύσις αὐτὴ διδάσκει ὑμᾶς ὅτι ἀνὴρ μὲν ἐὰν κομᾷ ἀτιμία αὐτῷ ἐστιν, ¹⁵ γυνὴ δὲ ἐὰν κομᾷ δόξα αὐτῇ ἐστιν; ὅτι ἡ κόμη ἀντὶ περιβολαίου δέδοται [αὐτῇ]. ¹⁶ Εἰ δέ τις δοκεῖ φιλόνεικος εἶναι, ἡμεῖς τοιαύτην συνήθειαν οὐκ ἔχομεν οὐδὲ αἱ ἐκκλησίαι τοῦ θεοῦ.

² Now I commend you because you remember me in everything and maintain the traditions even as I delivered them to you. ³ But I want you to understand that the head of every man is Christ, the head of a wife is her husband, and the head of Christ is God. ⁴ Every man who prays or prophesies with his head covered dishonors his head, ⁵ but every wife who prays or prophesies with her head uncovered dishonors her head, since it is the same as if her head were shaven. ⁶ For if a wife will not cover her head, then she should cut her hair short. But since it is disgraceful for a wife to cut off her hair or shave her head, let her cover her head. ⁷ For a man ought not to cover his head, since he is the image and glory of God, but woman is the glory of man. ⁸ For man was not made from woman, but woman from man. ⁹ Neither was man created for woman, but woman for man. ¹⁰ That is why a wife ought to have a symbol of authority on her head, because of the angels. ¹¹ Nevertheless, in the Lord woman is not independent of man nor man of woman; ¹² for as woman was made from man, so man is now born of woman. And all things are from God. ¹³ Judge for yourselves: is it proper for a wife to pray to God with her head uncovered? ¹⁴ Does not nature itself teach you that if a man wears long hair it is a disgrace for him, ¹⁵ but if a woman has long hair, it is her glory? For her hair is given to her for a covering. ¹⁶ If anyone is inclined to be contentious, we have no such practice, nor do the churches of God.

Table 4.1. The text of 1 Corinthians 11:2–16

Within the initial instructions given in 11:3–6, Paul states that Christ is the head of every man, the head of a wife is her husband, and the head of Christ is God (the Father; v. 3).[4] He goes on to provide a cultural application of this general principle when he declares that every man who prays or prophesies with his head covered dishonors his head (v. 4), and that every woman who prays or prophesies with her head uncovered dishonors her head (vv. 5–6).

It is at this point in the discussion that Paul substantiates his teaching by appeal to the creation texts of Genesis 1–2. In 1 Corinthians 11:7, Paul founds the headship of man and the corresponding command for men not to cover their heads on the understanding that men are created in the image and glory of God (Gen 1:26–27). Moreover, the required head covering for women derives from the woman being the glory of man (1 Cor 11:7). This understanding is made even more specific when Paul states that man was not made from woman, but woman from man (1 Cor 11:8; Gen 2:21–22). Moreover, Paul continues by noting that man was not created for woman, but rather woman for man (1 Cor 11:9; Gen 2:18, 20). Paul then summarizes his interpretation of the creation texts in Genesis 1–2 by stating that these texts serve as the foundation for the reason why a wife should have a symbol of authority on her head (1 Cor 11:10).[5] Thus, it is noteworthy that Paul's rationale

4. Regarding the contextual Greek use of the word for "head," see BDAG and the references mentioned above in note 44.

5. The Greek text may be rendered literally "the woman ought to have authority upon [her] head because of the angels" (διὰ τοῦτο ὀφείλει ἡ γυνὴ ἐξουσίαν ἔχειν ἐπὶ τῆς κεφαλῆς διὰ τοὺς ἀγγέλους). The phrase "on account of the angels" points toward the revelation of headship to Moses through mediating angels, elsewhere mentioned by Paul in Gal 3:19 (following Caird; cf. other positions in Thiselton, *1 Corinthians*, ad loc.). Once again, the revealed nature of male headship from the beginning mitigates against the feminist argument that these texts spoke to a limited social situation. Regarding the issue of veils, see the cultural background in Thiselton, *First Epistle to the Corinthians*, ad loc. Although his interpretation seems to bog down in the numerous and conflicting positions, Thiselton's presentation and evaluation of the Greek and Roman historical background proves helpful for understanding the historical context of the discussion on veils. While the universality of headship remains established as a tradition revealed from creation, its particular cultural expression

for teaching male headship is not founded on the fall (Gen 3), as many feminists and egalitarians would claim. Rather, he founds his understanding of the traditions entirely upon an interpretation of creation itself in Genesis 1–2. Therefore, Paul teaches from creation, not the fall, that male headship in marriage is normative. This founding of Paul's interpretation upon Genesis 1–2 suggests that the basic principles of his teaching are universal to the Christian church since they are based upon Scripture rather than Corinthian or Palestinian culture.

However, Paul qualifies his preceding interpretation and application with a clarifying statement in 1 Corinthians 11:11–12. It would be easy to take Paul's statements and overemphasize male headship to the point of a domineering autocracy in marriage, which does accord with the curse of the fall (Gen 3:16). To this misinterpretation of the norm and standard for the universal Christian community, Paul declares that woman is not independent of man, nor man of woman (v. 11). Just as woman was made from man, man is now born of woman and all things are from God (v. 12). In other words, within the context of male headship there is interdependence and men are dependent on women for help and completion. Men are not to make unilateral decisions or live like an autocratic ruler over their home. God gives a wife to man as a helpmate in order to provide balance and perspective, as well as to complete him (Gen 2:18, 20). This headship with interdependence is ordained by God (v. 12), and therefore it is a correction for those who would interpret Paul's statements in support of demeaning male domination over women.

Paul continues with a rhetorical question and asks whether or not it is proper for a wife to pray with her head uncovered, and then he appeals to nature and to the cultural convention of shorter hair for men and longer hair for women (1 Cor 11:13–15). However, Paul's final injunction is noteworthy: "If anyone is inclined to

---

changes from age to age, just as veils in Paul's day at Corinth indicated purity and devotion to one's husband. Veils were commended because their lack indicated a woman was not subordinate to a husband, and therefore men were free to proposition her.

be contentious, we have no such practice, nor do the churches of God" (1 Cor 11:16). Therefore, Paul indicates that the received and traditional interpretation of the creation passages in Genesis 1–2, which he outlined in the preceding verses, is universal among all the churches of God. This interpretation does not apply only to the Corinthian church and its specific situation at that time. Anyone who is contentious about Paul's interpretation not only departs from the practice of the early church, but they also depart from the norm of the universal church. In our present day, this implies that churches and Christian organizations who fail to recognize male headship in marriage have departed from authentic Christian teaching and practice, as well as from the universal (catholic) church. Any other interpretation is in serious error and creates division (*hairesis*).

In terms of reception history, Clement of Alexandria affirmed the value and moral responsibility of both men and women, yet due to the physical differences of the two affirms the woman's role in bearing children and maintaining the home.[6] After chronicling the similar abilities of both men and women, Clement goes on to enjoin male headship in the home and, contrary to egalitarian claims regarding the meaning of the word "head" (κεφαλὴ, *kephalē*) in antiquity, this Greek father states, "The ruling power is therefore the head."[7] Likewise, in commenting on the headship of Christ, Tertullian states explicitly, "The head he has here put for authority; now 'authority' will accrue to none else than the 'author.'"[8] In context, this headship extends to men, and Tertullian goes on to explain why Corinthian women should wear veils as a sign of humility and in order to obscure their beauty. According to the *Constitutions of the Holy Apostles* 1.3 regarding women, "Let the wife be obedient to her own proper husband, because 'the husband is the head of the wife.'"[9] Moreover, "'if the head of the wife be the man,' it is not reasonable that the rest of the body should

6. Clement of Alexandria, *Stromata* 4.8 (*ANF* 2:420).
7. Clement of Alexandria, *Stromata* 4.8 (*ANF* 2:420).
8. Tertullian, *Against Marcion* 5.8 (*ANF* 3:445).
9. *ANF* 7:394. Also see *Constitutions of the Holy Apostles* 1.3.8.

govern the head."[10] The *Constitutions of the Holy Apostles* continue by affirming that headship extends to church offices:

> Now, as to women's baptizing, we let you know that there is no small peril to those that undertake it. Therefore we do not advise you to it; for it is dangerous, or rather wicked and impious. For if the "man be the head of the woman," and he be originally ordained for the priesthood, it is not just to abrogate the order of the creation and leave the principal to come to the extreme part of the body. For the woman is the body of the man, taken from his side, and subject to him, from whom she was separated for the procreation of children. For says He, "He shall rule over thee." [Gen 3:16] For the principal part of the woman is the man, as being her head. But if in the foregoing constitutions we have not permitted them to teach, how will any one allow them, contrary to nature, to perform the office of a priest? For this is one of the ignorant practices of the Gentile atheism, to ordain women priests to the female deities, not one of the constitutions of Christ. For if baptism were to be administered by women, certainly our Lord would have been baptized by His own mother, and not by John; or when He sent us to baptize, He would have sent along with us women also for this purpose. But now He has nowhere, either by constitution or by writing, delivered to us any such thing; as knowing the order of nature, and the decency of the action; as being the Creator of nature, and the Legislator of the constitution.[11]

Therefore, the apostles and their disciples in the early centuries understood the New Testament to affirm male headship in marriage. Moreover, in relation to 1 Corinthians 11:2–16, the *Constitutions of the Holy Apostles* made the direct connection between male headship in the home and its direct extension to male headship in the church. These fathers took this stand over and against the common practice of ordaining female priestesses in the religions surrounding the church in its first centuries.

10. *Constitutions of the Holy Apostles* 3.1.6 (ANF 7:428).
11. *Constitutions of the Holy Apostles* 3.1.9 (ANF 7:429).

In commenting on the manner in which men are the image and glory of God, and in which woman is the glory of man (1 Cor 11:7–8; Gen 1:26–28; 2:18–25), St. Augustine writes that man as male and female were created in the image of God (Gen 1:26–28). However, Augustine understood 1 Corinthians 11:7–8 in relation to Genesis 2:18–25 to indicate that although man alone is the image of God, woman alone does not represent the image of God. It is only in relation to man that both male and female are the image of God.[12]

2. Creation and Relationship Applied in 1 Corinthians 14:33b–36

Again in 1 Corinthians 14:33b–36 Paul addresses the roles of men and women, and similar to 1 Timothy 2:11–15 this also occurs within an immediate context treating issues of ecclesiological order. In 1 Corinthians 14:33b–36 Paul commands women to remain silent in the churches since they are not permitted to speak. Rather, they are to be in submission "as the Law also says" (v. 34).[13] If there is anything they want to learn, they are to ask their husbands at home since "it is shameful for a woman to speak in church" (v. 35). Although Paul does not cite a specific passage from the Law, based on the reference to creation earlier in 1 Corinthians 11:2–16, and based on his appeals to creation in Ephesians 5:22–25 and 1 Timothy 2:11–15, it is likely that Paul has in mind the creation accounts in Genesis 1–2. It is less likely that Paul refers only to the authority of the male priesthood leading worship under the Mosaic covenant (e.g., Lev 8–10), or other similar passages, as a type or foreshadowing of worship under the antitype of the Christian covenant.

---

12. Augustine, *On the Holy Trinity* 7 (*NPNF* 1.3:158–60).

13. For a detailed exegetical treatment of this passage, see Carson, "'Silent in the Churches'"; Bordwine, *Pauline Doctrine of Male Headship*, 81–111. Cf. Keener, "Learning in the Assemblies."

1 Corinthians 14:33b–36
Ὡς ἐν πάσαις ταῖς ἐκκλησίαις τῶν ἁγίων [34] αἱ γυναῖκες ἐν ταῖς ἐκκλησίαις σιγάτωσαν· οὐ γὰρ ἐπιτρέπεται αὐταῖς λαλεῖν, ἀλλ᾽ ὑποτασσέσθωσαν, καθὼς καὶ ὁ νόμος λέγει. [35] εἰ δέ τι μαθεῖν θέλουσιν, ἐν οἴκῳ τοὺς ἰδίους ἄνδρας ἐπερωτάτωσαν· αἰσχρὸν γάρ ἐστιν γυναικὶ λαλεῖν ἐν ἐκκλησίᾳ. [36] ἢ ἀφ᾽ ὑμῶν ὁ λόγος τοῦ θεοῦ ἐξῆλθεν, ἢ εἰς ὑμᾶς μόνους κατήντησεν;
As in all the churches of the saints, [34] the women should keep silent in the churches. For they are not permitted to speak, but should be in submission, as the Law also says. [35] If there is anything they desire to learn, let them ask their husbands at home. For it is shameful for a woman to speak in church. [36] Or was it from you that the word of God came? Or are you the only ones it has reached?

Table 4.2. The text of 1 Corinthians 14:33b–36

However, Walter Kaiser attempts to deflect the issue by claiming that Paul's reference to the Law in 1 Corinthians 14:34 does not refer to the Pentateuch, but rather to Jewish oral tradition found in the Talmud.[14] Therefore, according to Kaiser's argument, Paul here quotes the Corinthians' question to him regarding rabbinic tradition and the practices of the early church. However, this view is to be rejected since Paul explicitly states "as the Law says," which is a standard quotation formula referring to the written Mosaic Law rather than to the oral tradition surrounding it (e.g., Matt 7:12; John 1:17; 1 Cor 9:8–9). Kaiser here allows his familiarity with later Jewish traditions, which define "the Law" as both the written Torah and oral Torah, to overshadow actual New Testament and Pauline usage in reference to the written Law only. Second, Kaiser's reference to the Talmud actually supports the complementarian position rather than his own. The Talmud is a written collection recording the rabbinic application of Mosaic Law. Therefore, the Talmud indicates that in Jewish circles of the early centuries AD passages such as Genesis 2:18–25 were received and understood to apply as outlined by Paul. Therefore, the Talmud *corroborates* Paul's reference to the Law and his specific application of Mosaic

14. Kaiser, "Paul, Women and the Church"; Kaiser, "Correcting Caricatures," 11–12.

texts regarding the roles of women in orderly worship. Although Kaiser asserts that the Law nowhere enjoins women to keep silent in the assemblies or churches, the Jewish community understood created roles as outlined in Genesis 1–2 to apply in this fashion. Following Warfield's detailed and nuanced account of inspiration, Paul was prepared by the Holy Spirit to give these instructions stemming from his Jewish instruction in the Law. God providentially prepared Paul to understand what it means for a woman to be a husband's "helper" within the churches, in alignment with Jewish reception history. The Talmud provides corroborating testimony that the Pauline instructions are a natural outflow and understanding of the significance of creation as male and female in Genesis 1–2. However, in contrast to the oral tradition recorded within the Talmud, the Pauline commands are inspired and avoid the excesses whereby women were not protected in marriage (e.g., Mishnaic divorce laws). Third, Kaiser argues the phrase "the women should keep silent in the churches" is a section heading topicalizing a correction of the Corinthian practice. However, if the full quotation extends to verse 35, then it is odd that there is neither discussion nor development following this two-verse heading. Thus, verses 34–35 break with the clear examples of Paul's references to a previous letter to the Corinthians, as in 1 Corinthians 7:1. In chapter 7, the section heading is given extended treatment in verses 2–40. It strikes one as odd that Paul would elsewhere provide a section heading followed by thirty-eight verses of explication, and then here provide a section heading with no development. Clearly, verses 34–35 function as a command specifying the nature of orderly worship in 14:26–40 rather than as a freestanding and contextless section heading.[15]

Moreover, immediate context indicates this prohibition is not restricted only to the Corinthian church since Paul states, "As in all the churches of the saints, the women should keep silent in the churches" (1 Cor 11:33b–34a). The phrase "as in all the churches of the saints" indicates that the practice of women remaining silent

15. Cf. MacGregor, "1 Corinthians 14:33b–38 as a Pauline Quotation-Refutation Device."

in the churches was universal within the early Christian community. Therefore, the argument that this command was a discrete response to a specific situation, error, or heresy arising within a few select churches is contradicted by the text itself. This was a universal practice.

Yet what does the phrase "the women should keep silent in the churches" mean? In context, they were not to ask questions publicly in Christian worship if there was something they wanted to learn (v. 35). Rather, they were to ask their husbands at home. As will be noted below, it is the husband's role to wash his wife in the word and sanctify her (Eph 5:22–25). Following Paul's statement, the act of not initiating a discussion of Scripture in public worship and instead asking her husband at home enabled the woman to "be in submission, as the Law also says" (1 Cor 14:34b).[16] Thus, a woman who restrained herself in public worship remained in submission to her husband and fulfilled the created purpose of serving as his help. This leads one to wonder whether passive and biblically ignorant men in our present age would dig into Scripture more deeply if their wife regularly asked them questions at home regarding its meaning rather than asking the pastor. Thus, they would begin to fulfill their calling as the priest in their home.

Moreover, Paul's use of the Law to substantiate this command indicates this practice of "remaining silent" was not based on social convention or the socioreligious setting of his day. Rather, this application was based upon an interpretation of the Five Books of Moses. Therefore, a straightforward reading of Scripture suggests that Paul's interpretation in 1 Corinthians 14:33b–36 is inspired, universally applicable, and, thus, authoritative today. It is not to be relegated to the bin of culturally limited historical curiosities in the New Testament.

Accordingly, we are left with a decision of whether to accede to the authority of Paul's inspired interpretation of the Law and his written instructions, or to ignore them. To those who choose not to

---

16. Regarding the limits of submission, and the unbiblical manner in which many women submit to men, see Moore, "Women, Stop Submitting to Men," 8–9.

acknowledge these instructions, Paul asks the rhetorical question, "Or was it from you that the word of God came? Or are you the only ones it has reached?" (v. 36). In other words, the inspired instruction of God came through the prophets and apostles and we are to accede to their authority. Furthermore, our present generation and churches are not the only ones the word of God has reached. We are commanded to listen to the wisdom of our fathers and remain in fellowship with the church of ages past by acknowledging Paul's instructions regarding the created roles of men and women within the church. The rise of the feminist and egalitarian movement in our present day is not the first challenge to these commands. Otherwise, Paul would never have written these instructions delineating the roles of men and women in marriage and the early church. If there was a challenge to male headship both in marriage and in the church in Paul's day, then the challenge to male headship within marriage and the church today likewise requires correction in order to experience full redemption in Jesus Christ and restoration to the created purpose of male and female.

In the reception history of this passage, the *Constitutions of the Holy Apostles* 3.1.6 declares, "We do not permit our 'women to teach in the church,' but only to pray and hear those that teach; for our Master and Lord, Jesus Himself, when He sent us the twelve to make disciples of the people and of the nations, did nowhere send out women to preach, although He did not want [lack] such."[17] Cyprian quotes both 1 Corinthians 14:34–35 and 1 Timothy 2:11–14 in concluding that women are to remain silent in the churches.[18] Tertullian recognizes the grounding of this binding instruction in Torah when commenting on women and silence in the church, for "he [Paul] goes to the law for his sanction that woman should be under obedience."[19] From this Pauline command to be silent in the churches, Tertullian opposed the false teacher who allowed women to baptize, and concluded that women should neither teach nor

17. *Constitutions of the Holy Apostles* 3.1.6 (*ANF* 7:427).

18. Cyprian, *Treatises* (*ANF* 5:546). Also see Chrysostom, *Homilies on First Corinthians* 37 (*NPNF* 1.12:222–25).

19. Tertullian, *Against Marcion* 5.8 (*ANF* 3:446).

baptize others.[20] Although some today argue that these commands apply only to wives, and that it is necessary for single women to serve in leadership positions, to teach, and to preach on the mission field, Tertullian concludes otherwise that "on the ground of her position, nothing in the way of public honour is permitted to a virgin."[21] Or in other words, Tertullian understood Scripture to mean that single women were not allowed to lead men.

3. Galatians 3:28 in Literary Context

In addition to the examples of Deborah and Huldah from the Old Testament, mentioned above, egalitarians often cite Galatians 3:28 in order to argue that gender roles have been abolished for the Christian church since Christ reversed the fall: "There is neither Jew nor Greek, there is neither slave nor free, there is neither male nor female, for you are all one in Christ Jesus." However, there are several problems with this interpretation.[22]

Galatians 3:26–29
[26] Πάντες γὰρ υἱοὶ θεοῦ ἐστε διὰ τῆς πίστεως ἐν Χριστῷ Ἰησοῦ· [27] ὅσοι γὰρ εἰς Χριστὸν ἐβαπτίσθητε, Χριστὸν ἐνεδύσασθε. [28] οὐκ ἔνι Ἰουδαῖος οὐδὲ Ἕλλην, οὐκ ἔνι δοῦλος οὐδὲ ἐλεύθερος, οὐκ ἔνι ἄρσεν καὶ θῆλυ· πάντες γὰρ ὑμεῖς εἷς ἐστε ἐν Χριστῷ Ἰησοῦ. [29] εἰ δὲ ὑμεῖς Χριστοῦ, ἄρα τοῦ Ἀβραὰμ σπέρμα ἐστέ, κατ᾽ ἐπαγγελίαν κληρονόμοι.
[26] for in Christ Jesus you are all sons of God, through faith. [27] For as many of you as were baptized into Christ have put on Christ. [28] There is neither Jew nor Greek, there is neither slave nor free, there is no male and female, for you are all one in Christ Jesus. [29] And if you are Christ's, then you are Abraham's offspring, heirs according to promise.

Table 4.3. The text of Galatians 3:26–29

20. Tertullian, *On Baptism* 17 (*ANF* 3:677).

21. Tertullian, *On the Veiling of Virgins* 9 (*ANF* 4:33).

22. See Bordwine, *Pauline Doctrine of Male Headship*, 257–68; Elliott, "Jesus Movement Was Not Egalitarian"; Walden, "Galatians 3:28." Cf. Fee, "Male and Female in the New Creation."

First, it is preferable to interpret a given verse within its literary context. Within the book of Galatians, Paul deals with the issue of Gentiles being compelled to observe the ceremonial law rather than trusting completely in justification by faith alone. Therefore, the book as a whole may be classified as soteriological in nature. The immediate literary context of Galatians 3:28 bears this out:

> Now before faith came we were held captive under the law, imprisoned until the coming faith would be revealed. So then, the law was our guardian until Christ came, in order that we might be *justified by faith*. But now that faith has come, we are no longer under a guardian, for in Christ Jesus you are all sons of God, through faith. For as many of you as were baptized into Christ have put on Christ. *There is neither Jew nor Greek, there is neither slave nor free, there is neither male nor female, for you are all one in Christ Jesus.* And if you are Christ's, then you are Abraham's offspring, heirs according to the promise. (Gal 3:23–29)

Thus, we see that the breaking down of boundaries teaches the extension of justification by faith across boundaries of race, social standing, and sex. The separation by race and gender for worship in the courts of the temple under the old covenant no longer applies to justification under the new, and no segment of society is to be excluded from baptism in Christ. Moreover, both Jew and Greek, slave and free, as well as male and female are one in Christ Jesus in the sense that they are all now Abraham's offspring and heirs to the promise (v. 29). Therefore, Galatians 3:28 does not refer to roles within marriage (i.e., anthropology) or within the church (i.e., ecclesiology). Rather, it is defining the nature and extent of salvation in response to the Judaizing soteriological heresy in Galatia.

Second, whereas the book of Galatians is soteriological in nature, Paul's explicit statement prohibiting women from teaching or holding positions of authority over men within the church occurs in 1 Timothy, discussed below, which treats predominantly ecclesiological issues. Therefore, contextually, 1 Timothy refers to appropriate church order, whereas Galatians does not. To interpret and apply a soteriological statement out of context in order to nullify an explicit ecclesiological statement violates normal interpretive conventions. This approach severs contextual meaning and authorial intent in the attempt to wrestle the Bible to conform to contemporary ideology and the spirit of the times. Consequently, Galatians 3:28 may not legitimately be pitted against 1 Timothy 2:11–15 and other passages since Galatians 3:28 does not refer to gender roles within the church. To the contrary, Paul's other writings do refer to gender roles specifically, and thus Paul's instructions for men and women within the family and within the church stand.

Third, based on the cumulative argument to this point, this verse does not refer to the abolition of gender roles on the basis of Christ's reversal of the fall since the created roles of men and women both within marriage and in the church do not derive from the fall. Rather, the role distinctions outlined by Paul (1 Cor 11:2–16; 14:33a–36; Eph 5:22–25; 1 Tim 2:11–15) derive from Paul's inspired interpretation of Genesis 1–2. Therefore, we must seek a contextual interpretation of Galatians 3:28 which is both faithful to its immediate literary context and also remains consistent with Paul's other writings. Thus, the feminist interpretation of this verse runs counter to the immediate literary context in Galatians, whereas the complementarian position does not. In the end, pitting Galatians 3:28 against 1 Timothy 2:11–15 undermines the traditional Reformed and conservative evangelical doctrine of Scripture. Paul becomes a confused man who advocates contradictory positions in Scripture, and his exegesis of Moses must be deemed errant rather than inspired. Given an egalitarian reading, the human element overrides the divine will in the composition of Scripture, and hinders its *theopneustic* intent, clarity, and consistency.

In contrast, the present reading of Galatians 3:28 accords with patristic reception. Ignatius quotes Galatians 3:28 in support of his teaching of one Eucharist for all since "there is one nature, and one family of mankind."[23] Similarly, Clement of Alexandria exhorted the nations, and based his call on this verse since Christ

---

23. Ignatius, *Epistle to the Philadelphians* 6 (*ANF* 1:81).

is not divided and all may be transformed by God's Holy Spirit.[24] Hyppolytus alludes to this verse in his refutation of the Naassene system of thought, which carried this verse beyond a soteriological understanding to an abolition of all distinction between the sexes in advocating emasculation so that men would become hermaphrodites.[25] St. Chrysostom likewise understands this verse to refer to salvation when he quotes Paul's teaching that everyone who calls on the name of the Lord will be saved, and then substantiates this quote by appeal to Romans 3:28 and its teaching that salvation crosses all human boundaries.[26] St. Jerome emphasizes that the distinction between the sexes is necessary for marriage, quotes Galatians 3:28, and then remarks that the distinction between the sexes will only be abolished when both men and women become like the angels at glorification.[27] St. Augustine quoted this verse in order to demonstrate that spiritual grace extends to all, and indicated it referred only to the second birth and did not abolish the created divisions of the first birth.[28]

4. Creation and Relationship Applied in Ephesians 5:21–33 and Colossians 3:18–19

Within Paul's teaching on the structure and purpose of family roles in Ephesians 5:21–33, Paul cites Genesis 2:24, "Therefore a man shall leave his father and mother and hold fast to his wife, and the two shall become one flesh." This grounding of marital roles in a creation text suggests that (1) God established these roles from creation

24. Clement of Alexandria, *Exhortation to the Heathen* 11 (*ANF* 2:203). Also see Homily 30 on Rom 15:25–27 and Homily 12.12 on 1 Corinthians.

25. Hyppolytus, *Refutation of All Heresies* 5.2 (*ANF* 5:49).

26. Chrysostom, *Commentary on the Acts of the Apostles*, Homily 10 on Acts 2:14 (*NPNF* 1.11).

27. Jerome, *Letter LXXV To Theodora* 2 (*NPNF* 2.6:155).

28. Augustine, *Confessions* 13.23.33 (*NPNF* 1.1:201); Augustine, *Writings in Connection with the Manichaean Controversy* 24.1 (*NPNF* 1.4:317); Augustine, *Lectures or Tractates on the Gospel According to St. John Chapter XVII.21–23*, Tractate 110.2 (*NPNF* 1.7:409).

and (2) these commands remain universal throughout creation and are not limited to the discrete social situation at Ephesus.[29]

Ephesians 5:21–33
[21] Ὑποτασσόμενοι ἀλλήλοις ἐν φόβῳ Χριστοῦ, [22] αἱ γυναῖκες τοῖς ἰδίοις ἀνδράσιν [Byzantine/Majority text ὑποτάσσεσθε] ὡς τῷ κυρίῳ, [23] ὅτι ἀνήρ ἐστιν κεφαλὴ τῆς γυναικὸς ὡς καὶ ὁ Χριστὸς κεφαλὴ τῆς ἐκκλησίας, αὐτὸς σωτὴρ τοῦ σώματος· [24] ἀλλ᾽ ὡς ἡ ἐκκλησία ὑποτάσσεται τῷ Χριστῷ, οὕτως καὶ αἱ γυναῖκες τοῖς ἀνδράσιν ἐν παντί. [25] Οἱ ἄνδρες, ἀγαπᾶτε τὰς γυναῖκας, καθὼς καὶ ὁ Χριστὸς ἠγάπησεν τὴν ἐκκλησίαν καὶ ἑαυτὸν παρέδωκεν ὑπὲρ αὐτῆς, [26] ἵνα αὐτὴν ἁγιάσῃ καθαρίσας τῷ λουτρῷ τοῦ ὕδατος ἐν ῥήματι, [27] ἵνα παραστήσῃ αὐτὸς ἑαυτῷ ἔνδοξον τὴν ἐκκλησίαν, μὴ ἔχουσαν σπίλον ἢ ῥυτίδα ἤ τι τῶν τοιούτων, ἀλλ᾽ ἵνα ᾖ ἁγία καὶ ἄμωμος. [28] οὕτως ὀφείλουσιν [καὶ] οἱ ἄνδρες ἀγαπᾶν τὰς ἑαυτῶν γυναῖκας ὡς τὰ ἑαυτῶν σώματα. ὁ ἀγαπῶν τὴν ἑαυτοῦ γυναῖκα ἑαυτὸν ἀγαπᾷ. [29] Οὐδεὶς γάρ ποτε τὴν ἑαυτοῦ σάρκα ἐμίσησεν ἀλλ᾽ ἐκτρέφει καὶ θάλπει αὐτήν, καθὼς καὶ ὁ Χριστὸς τὴν ἐκκλησίαν, [30] ὅτι μέλη ἐσμὲν τοῦ σώματος αὐτοῦ. [31] ἀντὶ τούτου καταλείψει ἄνθρωπος [τὸν] πατέρα καὶ [τὴν] μητέρα καὶ προσκολληθήσεται πρὸς τὴν γυναῖκα αὐτοῦ, καὶ ἔσονται οἱ δύο εἰς σάρκα μίαν. [32] τὸ μυστήριον τοῦτο μέγα ἐστίν· ἐγὼ δὲ λέγω εἰς Χριστὸν καὶ εἰς τὴν ἐκκλησίαν. [33] πλὴν καὶ ὑμεῖς οἱ καθ᾽ ἕνα, ἕκαστος τὴν ἑαυτοῦ γυναῖκα οὕτως ἀγαπάτω ὡς ἑαυτόν, ἡ δὲ γυνὴ ἵνα φοβῆται τὸν ἄνδρα.

[21] submitting to one another out of reverence for Christ. [22] Wives, submit to your own husbands, as to the Lord. [23] For the husband is the head of the wife even as Christ is the head of the church, his body, and is himself its Savior. [24] Now as the church submits to Christ, so also wives should submit in everything to their husbands. [25] Husbands, love your wives, as Christ loved the church and gave himself up for her, [26] that he might sanctify her, having cleansed her by the washing of water with the word, [27] so that he might present the church to himself in splendor, without spot or wrinkle or any such thing, that she might be holy and without blemish. [28] In the same way husbands should love their wives as their own bodies. He who loves his wife loves himself. [29] For no one ever hated his own flesh, but nourishes and cherishes it, just as Christ does the church, [30] because we are members of his body. [31] "Therefore a man shall leave his father and mother and hold fast to his wife, and the two shall become one flesh."

Table 4.4. The text of Ephesians 5:21–33

29. For a more detailed presentation, see Knight, "Husbands and Wives as Analogues"; Bordwine, *Pauline Doctrine of Male Headship*, 112–48; Croteau, "'To Make Her Holy' (Ephesians 5:26)." Cf. Marshall, "Mutual Love and Submission in Marriage." Fee, "Cultural Context of Ephesians 5:18—6:9."

If one follows the eclectic Greek text tradition (NA28 or UBS5), the opening participle of this unit ("submitting to one another out of reverence for Christ") in Ephesians 5:21 follows a series of participles dependent on the imperative "be filled with the Spirit" in verse 18. Not only does the teaching of this unit regarding the roles and relationships in marriage point toward the manner for living the Spirit-filled life, but it also follows the command to be imitators of God in (v. 1) and the command to examine carefully how we walk (v. 15). Therefore, Paul's instructions for marriage in 5:21–33 flow from the earlier commands to imitate God, to make sure we walk wisely when the days are evil, and to be filled with the Spirit. We are to submit to one another alongside singing praise and giving thanks to God as part of the Spirit-filled life. The instructions in 5:22–33 specify how we are to submit to one another, which is commanded in 5:21. However, if one follows Codex Sinaiticus (υποτασσεσθωσαν, *hupotassesthōsan*) or the Byzantine tradition (ὑποτάσσεσθε, *hupotassesthe*), then the paragraph begins in 5:22 with the verbal command for wives to submit to their husbands.

Paul specifies what he means by "submitting to one another" when he instructs wives to submit to their husbands (v. 22) since the husband is the head of the wife as Christ is the head of the church (v. 23). Analogous to the submission of the church to Christ is the submission of the wife to the husband in everything (v. 24). Moreover, men are then commanded to love their wives as Christ loved the church and gave himself up for her (v. 25) in order to sanctify her by the washing of water with the word and to present her holy and without blemish (vv. 26–27). Following this pattern, the husband is to love his wife as his own body (vv. 28–30). Within this context of male headship and the submission of the wife to the husband, analogous to the submission of the church to Christ and Christ's sanctification of the church, Paul then quotes Genesis 2:24 in order to make the point that it is a mystery how the two become one flesh analogous to Christ and the church (vv. 31–32). Paul then concludes the address to husbands and wives by instructing the husband to love his wife as himself, and the wife to respect her husband (v. 33).

The creation basis of Paul's command for the husband to love his wife as himself and for the wife to submit herself to her husband is evidenced by Paul's quotation of Genesis 2:24. The citation of this verse suggests that this analogy of Christ and the church and these instructions are rooted in creation. The submission of the wife to the husband and the husband's role of loving his wife, sanctifying her by the washing of the word, and nourishing and cherishing her are thus understood to be an interpretation and application of Genesis 2:24, which Paul held in mind as he composed this unit.

Therefore, since this unit is rooted in creation, the submission of the wife to her husband (Eph 5:22) and the headship of the husband over his wife (v. 23) do not derive from the fall. Rather, they are part of the created order and the redemptive goal for the sanctified life. This is the fulfillment of becoming one flesh (v. 31). Restoration in Christ therefore calls wives to turn from fallen patterns of unsubmissive rebellion and husbands to turn from a fallen pattern of self-centered and unsanctified petty dictatorship. Indeed, it is impossible to be imitators of God (Eph 5:1), to live the Spirit-filled life (v. 18), or to exemplify the analogous relationship of Christ to the church (vv. 25–30) if we fail to submit to Paul's teaching regarding what it means to be "one flesh" (Gen 2:24). Indeed, becoming "one flesh" entails a wife submitting to her husband's headship, and it entails the husband following Christ's pattern of self-sacrificial love for the church as the husband sanctifies, nourishes, and cherishes his wife.[30] Just as Christ submitted to the Father, husbands are called to live in full submission to the Father's will. Just as Christ loved the church by giving himself, husbands

30. Many egalitarians debate the meaning of the Greek word for "head, headship," break with its traditional interpretation, and argue it instead means "origin, source." For example, see Mowczko, "*Kephalē* and 'Male Headship' in Paul's Letters," and the writings she recommends (https://margmowczko.com/kephale-and-male-headship-in-pauls-letters/). However, Wayne Grudem argues more persuasively from accepted methods of semantic analysis in his direct appeal to Greek contextual usage and lexicography than subsequent egalitarian critics ("Does κεφαλὴ ['Head'] Mean 'Source'").

are called to love their wives by being fully given to taking care of the needs of their wives. Whereas many a husband remains biblically ignorant and at some level views Christianity as feminine, his chief calling in Christ is to sanctify and cleanse her with Scripture that she may be spotless and without blemish. This assumes a loving manner (1 Cor 13) rather than a harsh, heavy-handed, or domineering application of Scripture that is totally lacking in gentleness or sensitivity.

The parallel and abbreviated passage in Colossians 3:18–19 does not cite Genesis 2:24. However, it states in straightforward fashion that wives are to submit to their husbands "as is fitting in the Lord," and husbands are to love their wives without being harsh to them. Thus, the phrase "as is fitting in the Lord" in verse 18 indicates that male headship in marriage is not abrogated under the Christian covenant. Rather, Paul here affirms male headship within the church age. Moreover, the phrase "as is fitting in the Lord" implies that submission remains a Christian ideal, and wives are not called to submit to sin or disobedience. Paul then balances this instruction in verse 19 by teaching that men should not be harsh toward their wives. Thus, the submission of the wife and the thoughtful leadership of the husband follow the pattern of creation, and they are the redemptive goal of sanctification from fallen patterns of either the wife's rebellion or the husband's ruthless domination over her.

In terms of reception history, Clement of Alexandria affirms the similar abilities of men and women, yet quotes both from Ephesians 2:21–33 and Colossians 3:18–19 in affirming male headship in the home. Although egalitarians quibble over the meaning of the Greek word for "head," Clement, himself a Greek speaker and writer, specifically states, "The ruling power is therefore the head."[31] Tertullian likewise affirmed the submission of a wife to her husband when referencing this passage as an example of how a New Testament command affirms Old Testament Law.[32] In his

31. Clement of Alexandria, *Stromata* 4.8 (*ANF* 2:420). Also see *Instructor* 3.12 (*ANF* 2:294).

32. Tertullian, *Against Marcion* 5.18 (*ANF* 3:468). Also see Ignatius, *Epistle*

homily on Ephesians 5:22–24, Chrysostom identifies the role of the man as head in terms of authority, and speaks of the woman's role as submission to her husband as unto God.[33] Chrysostom balances this interpretation by applying Paul's call for husbands to love their wives as Christ loves the church, similar to the teaching of St. Augustine.[34] Elsewhere, Augustine follows Ephesians 5:23 and Colossians 3:18 in maintaining "man is subject to Christ, and the woman is subject to the man."[35]

5. Creation and Relationship Applied in 1 Timothy 2:8–15

Whereas the previous two passages under discussion applied to the roles and attitudes of men and women in marriage, 1 Timothy 2:11–15 moves outward and addresses the role of women within the Christian community at large (ecclesiology).[36] Within 1 Timothy, Paul provides guidelines for Timothy in leading and establishing well-ordered Christian communities, and once again we find that Paul's thought on the role of men and women centers upon

---

to the Philadelphians 4 (*ANF* 1:81); Chrysostom, *Homilies on Ephesians* 1 (*NPNF* 1.13:50); St. Chrysostom, *Homilies on First Corinthians* 26 (*NPNF* 1.12:151); Ambrose, *Exposition of the Christian Faith* 13.156 (*NPNF* 2.10:303).

33. Chrysostom, *Homilies on Ephesians* 20 (*NPNF* 1.13:144); Chrysostom, *Homilies on Colossians* 10 (Col 3:18–25) (*NPNF* 1.13:304).

34. Augustine, *On Continence* (*NPNF* 1.3:388).

35. Augustine, *Our Lord's Sermon on the Mount* 12 (*NPNF* 1.6:16); Augustine, *Sermons on Selected Lessons of the New Testament* (*NPNF* 1.6:249); Augustine, *On Marriage and Concupiscence* 10 (*NPNF* 1.5:267).

36. For a detailed exegetical discussion of this passage, see Moo, "What Does It Mean Not to Teach?"; Köstenberger and Schreiner, *Women in the Church*; Bordwine, *Pauline Doctrine of Male Headship*, 149–95; Köstenberger, "Syntax of 1 Timothy 2:12." With regard to application for single women, see McCulley, "When You Don't Have a Better Half." Cf. Kroeger and Kroeger, *I Suffer Not a Woman*; Belleville, "Teaching and Usurping Authority"; Davis, "Incarnation, Trinity, and the Ordination of Women"; Brown, "A Historian Looks at 1 Timothy 2:11–14"; Foster, "1 Timothy 2:8–15 and Gender Wars"; Hübner, "Translating Αὐθεντέω (Authenteō) in 1 Timothy 2:12a"; Hübner, "Revisiting the Clarity of Scripture in 1 Timothy 2:12."

the early chapters of Genesis when he alludes both to creation and the fall in 1 Timothy 2:13–14 as biblical warrant for his preceding instructions.

Within this unit, Paul begins by instructing men to pray in every place by lifting holy hands without anger or quarrelling (1 Tim 2:8). From the outset, therefore, the feminist claim that biblical submission leads to abuse is countered by the first command in the foremost passage under dispute: men are required to pray, lifting holy hands "without anger or quarrelling." A husband who loves his wife like Christ loves the church (Eph 5:22–33) and who prays without anger or quarrelling cannot be abusive or demeaning toward his wife while himself remaining submitted to God. Every time faithful pastors preach this passage and touch on this theme, this command constrains everything which follows.

Conversely, women are to dress modestly and be self-controlled rather than dressing in an expensive fashion since modesty befits a godly woman who performs good works (vv. 9–10). Moreover, Paul instructs women to learn quietly from the teaching "with all submissiveness" (v. 11). This reference to submissiveness could mean the submission of a married woman toward her husband or of all women to Scripture, but presumably it refers to both. Furthermore, this reference to "woman" may refer ambiguously either to a single or to a married woman, and presumably it refers to both since it is not qualified. Then Paul continues by stating that he does not permit a woman to teach or to exercise authority over a man (v. 12).[37]

37. Kaiser argues that Paul's command for women not to teach was given temporarily during Nero's persecution ("Women, Paul and the Church," 11). However, he fails to explain the historical relationship between women teaching and the persecution. In the light of Paul's other clear statements on the roles of women, this argument remains specious at best.

1 Timothy 2:8–15
[8] Βούλομαι οὖν προσεύχεσθαι τοὺς ἄνδρας ἐν παντὶ τόπῳ ἐπαίροντας ὁσίους χεῖρας χωρὶς ὀργῆς καὶ διαλογισμοῦ. [9] Ὡσαύτως [καὶ] γυναῖκας ἐν καταστολῇ κοσμίῳ μετὰ αἰδοῦς καὶ σωφροσύνης κοσμεῖν ἑαυτάς, μὴ ἐν πλέγμασιν καὶ χρυσίῳ ἢ μαργαρίταις ἢ ἱματισμῷ πολυτελεῖ, [10] ἀλλ᾽ ὃ πρέπει γυναιξὶν ἐπαγγελλομέναις θεοσέβειαν, δι᾽ ἔργων ἀγαθῶν. [11] Γυνὴ ἐν ἡσυχίᾳ μανθανέτω ἐν πάσῃ ὑποταγῇ· [12] διδάσκειν δὲ γυναικὶ οὐκ ἐπιτρέπω οὐδὲ αὐθεντεῖν ἀνδρός, ἀλλ᾽ εἶναι ἐν ἡσυχίᾳ. [13] Ἀδὰμ γὰρ πρῶτος ἐπλάσθη, εἶτα Εὔα. [14] καὶ Ἀδὰμ οὐκ ἠπατήθη, ἡ δὲ γυνὴ ἐξαπατηθεῖσα ἐν παραβάσει γέγονεν· [15] σωθήσεται δὲ διὰ τῆς τεκνογονίας, ἐὰν μείνωσιν ἐν πίστει καὶ ἀγάπῃ καὶ ἁγιασμῷ μετὰ σωφροσύνης·
[8] I desire then that in every place the men should pray, lifting holy hands without anger or quarreling; [9] likewise also that women should adorn themselves in respectable apparel, with modesty and self-control, not with braided hair and gold or pearls or costly attire, [10] but with what is proper for women who profess godliness—with good works. [11] Let a woman learn quietly with all submissiveness. [12] I do not permit a woman to teach or to exercise authority over a man; rather, she is to remain quiet. [13] For Adam was formed first, then Eve; [14] and Adam was not deceived, but the woman was deceived and became a transgressor. [15] Yet she will be saved through childbearing—if they continue in faith and love and holiness, with self-control.

Table 4.5. The text of 1 Timothy 2:8–15

This prohibition of women teaching or exercising authority over men is the point where the contemporary church and para-church organizations commonly resist Paul's instructions in at least two ways.[38] First, some argue that this instruction was bound to that specific time and place and that it was not a universal instruction. Second, others argue that a patriarchal society is derivative of the fall, which is reversed in Christ, citing Galatians 3:28 (discussed above). This approach runs counter to the cumulative argument of the present discussion that the creation of male headship and the woman as Adam's helpmate are rooted in creation rather than the fall.

38. Biblically, it is decidedly not the case that women are forbidden to minister. For example, see Susan Hunt, "Women's Ministry in the Local Church"; Ortlund, "Sweet Sacrifices."

In response to the first objection, it is noteworthy that Paul begins this unit in verse 8 by stating, "I desire then that *in every place* the men should pray . . ." Therefore, from the outset of this paragraph the scope of Paul's command is every place where Christian believers gather together for worship, instruction, and fellowship. The following instructions for women are linked to this verse by the word "likewise" (ὡσαύτος, *hōsautos*), which indicates that the universal scope of the preceding verse applies with the following instructions to women. Therefore, Paul's instructions for women not to teach or exercise authority over men are not bound to a specific situation with which Timothy was dealing at one discrete time and in one location. Rather, this command is universal for all believers in all times and in all places.

In response to the second objection, Paul substantiates his instruction for women not to teach or exercise authority over men by immediately mentioning creation: "For Adam was formed first, then Eve" (v. 13).[39] This allusion refers to God's creation of Adam preceding Eve in Genesis 2:18–25. This sequence of man preceding woman and the narrative to which it refers therefore alludes to the role of woman as the helpmate of man. Thus, Paul understood the act of creation and the created purpose of woman as man's helpmate to apply to the church. In particular, since woman is to be man's helpmate, women are restricted from teaching men or holding any position of authority over them. Then Paul continues by appealing to the Fall Narrative (Gen 3:1–24) when he states that "Adam was not deceived, but the woman was deceived and became a transgressor." Biblical and human history is replete with examples of male sin, yet Paul's inspired and authoritative interpretation of the fall indicates that male headship and the restriction of the teaching office and positions of authority to men somehow preserves a balance that was lost when the woman was deceived with the fall. This would suggest that allowing women to teach and hold a position of authority over men, and especially the present tendency to encourage this, perpetuates Eve's act of taking the initiative with Adam. Precisely at this point Eve took the initiative to lead Adam contrary to the Lord God's command, and she did

---

39. Wolters, "Semantic Study of αὐθέντης."

not content herself as his helpmate. Therefore, Paul substantiates his instructions for women not to teach or hold a position of authority over men by appeal to creation in Genesis 2, and the allusion to the fall narrative does not indicate that these instructions are the result of the curse following the fall. Rather, a woman teaching or holding a position of authority both departs from the created role of helpmate and perpetuates the fall by mimicking the act of Eve, who led Adam rather than submitting to him.

Paul then closes this unit by stating that the godly woman "will be saved through childbearing—if they continue in faith and love and holiness, with self-control" (v. 15). One of the primary ways in which woman serves as man's helpmate is in the raising of children, in which role the prototypical woman possesses a capacity for patiently nurturing children that is far beyond that of the typical man. However, this is not a blind promise that a woman will be saved by having children. Rather, she must follow Paul's instructions by continuing in faith and love and holiness, with the self-control to avoid vain displays of beauty and wealth, and with the self-control to submit herself to the role of a helpmate rather than striving for the position of headship by teaching or holding authority over men. Moreover, this text remains an implicit call for men to lead rather than abdicating roles of leadership and teaching so that women must step forward like Deborah or Huldah in times of moral darkness.

How did the early church understand this text? After mentioning a baptismal heresy introduced by a woman in his churches, Tertullian alludes to 2 Timothy 2:11–12 in declaring that she had no right to teach even sound doctrine.[40] Tertullian elsewhere indicates that neither married women nor virgins are permitted to teach, baptize, perform any manly function, or to hold sacerdotal office.[41] Cyprian appealed to 1 Timothy 2:11–14 as proof for women remaining silent in the church.[42] In his homily on 2 Timothy 2:11–15, St. Chrysostom emphasizes the quietness of women in church, the prohibition against them teaching, and their prescribed role in childbearing

40. Tertullian, *On Baptism* 1 (*ANF* 3:669).

41. Tertullian, *On the Veiling of Virgins* 9 (*ANF* 4:33).

42. Cyprian, *Treatises* (*ANF* 5:546); also see Cyril, *Procatechesis* (*NPNF* 2.7:4).

and bringing up children.[43] The female quest for authority in the church has existed since the first centuries, which led Chrysostom to remind his readers of Paul's injunction against women speaking in church or teaching.[44] St. Jerome records one account of a woman keen to study Scripture who carefully regulated her speech in order to obey Paul's command that a woman not teach.[45]

6. Appeal to the Patriarchal Narrative in 1 Peter 3:1–7

The final New Testament passage referring to the Pentateuch as the foundational text for understanding the roles of husbands and wives is 1 Peter 3:1–7.[46] This passage, however, refers to the positive example of Sarah and Abraham within the patriarchal narratives (Gen 18:12) rather than to creation as the ground for the ethical command. Thus, Peter chooses one of the episodes where the patriarchal family set a good example for the following generations, rather than an example of familial unfaithfulness demonstrating the need for covenant, as with polygamy in Genesis 16 and 28–36.

Within this passage, Peter instructs wives to be subject to their husbands, so that even if he is an unbeliever, he may be won by the conduct of his wife (vv. 1–2). It is significant that this verb ὑποτασσόμεναι (hupotassomenai, "being submissive") is a feminine plural present passive participle, which suggests that women are to be submissive or to submit themselves rather than their husbands demanding submission or behaving in a domineering fashion over them. Submission is not forced; it is freely given. Therefore, submission is the woman's responsibility, not the man's. Peter continues by urging wives not to

43. Chrysostom, *Homilies on 1 Timothy* 9 (*NPNF* 1.13:435–37).

44. Chrysostom, *Treatise Concerning the Christian Priesthood* 3 (*NPNF* 1.9:49); Chrysostom, *Homilies on Titus* (*NPNF* 1.13:532).

45. Jerome, *To Principia* (*NPNF* 2.6:255–56).

46. For a detailed exegetical treatment, see Grudem, "Wives Like Sarah." Regarding application, see Harris, "Word to Husbands"; Barrett, "God's Design for Marriage." Cf. Davids, "Silent Witness in Marriage"; Nugent, "'Weaker Sex' or a Weak Translation?"

concern themselves with external beauty, but rather to be concerned with adorning themselves with the imperishable beauty of a gentle and quiet spirit, which is precious in God's sight (vv. 3–4). Peter next substantiates these instructions by noting that the holy women of old adorned themselves by submitting to their husbands, and he refers to Sarah respectfully calling her husband "lord" (Gen 18:12). Conversely, Peter instructs husbands to live with their wives in an understanding manner and to show them honor lest their prayers be hindered (v. 7). Therefore, these instructions for marriage are not one-sided. Weight falls upon the Christian husband to honor his wife if he wants his prayers to be heard. Anything less than honoring his wife fails to meet the standard of the redeemed Christian concept of marriage.

1 Peter 3:1–7

[1] Ὁμοίως αἱ γυναῖκες, ὑποτασσόμεναι τοῖς ἰδίοις ἀνδράσιν, ἵνα καὶ εἴ τινες ἀπειθοῦσιν τῷ λόγῳ, διὰ τῆς τῶν γυναικῶν ἀναστροφῆς ἄνευ λόγου κερδηθήσονται [2] ἐποπτεύσαντες τὴν ἐν φόβῳ ἁγνὴν ἀναστροφὴν ὑμῶν. [3] ὧν ἔστω οὐχ ὁ ἔξωθεν ἐμπλοκῆς τριχῶν καὶ περιθέσεως χρυσίων ἢ ἐνδύσεως ἱματίων κόσμος, [4] ἀλλ᾽ ὁ κρυπτὸς τῆς καρδίας ἄνθρωπος ἐν τῷ ἀφθάρτῳ τοῦ πραέως καὶ ἡσυχίου πνεύματος ὅ ἐστιν ἐνώπιον τοῦ θεοῦ πολυτελές. [5] οὕτως γάρ ποτε καὶ αἱ ἅγιαι γυναῖκες αἱ ἐλπίζουσαι εἰς θεὸν ἐκόσμουν ἑαυτὰς ὑποτασσόμεναι τοῖς ἰδίοις ἀνδράσιν, [6] ὡς Σάρρα ὑπήκουσεν τῷ Ἀβραὰμ κύριον αὐτὸν καλοῦσα ἧς ἐγενήθητε τέκνα ἀγαθοποιοῦσαι καὶ μὴ φοβούμεναι μηδεμίαν πτόησιν. [7] Οἱ ἄνδρες ὁμοίως, συνοικοῦντες κατὰ γνῶσιν ὡς ἀσθενεστέρῳ σκεύει τῷ γυναικείῳ, ἀπονέμοντες τιμὴν ὡς καὶ συγκληρονόμοις χάριτος ζωῆς εἰς τὸ μὴ ἐγκόπτεσθαι τὰς προσευχὰς ὑμῶν.

[1] Likewise, wives, be subject to your own husbands, so that even if some do not obey the word, they may be won without a word by the conduct of their wives, [2] when they see your respectful and pure conduct. [3] Do not let your adorning be external—the braiding of hair and the putting on of gold jewelry, or the clothing you wear—[4] but let your adorning be the hidden person of the heart with the imperishable beauty of a gentle and quiet spirit, which in God's sight is very precious. [5] For this is how the holy women who hoped in God used to adorn themselves, by submitting to their own husbands, [6] as Sarah obeyed Abraham, calling him lord. And you are her children, if you do good and do not fear anything that is frightening. [7] Likewise, husbands, live with your wives in an understanding way, showing honor to the woman as the weaker vessel, since they are heirs with you the grace of life, so that your prayers may not be hindered.

Table 4.6. The text of 1 Peter 3:1–7

Moreover, these instructions for husbands and wives are found in the larger book context of the initial address at the beginning of Peter's letter: "Peter, an apostle of Jesus Christ, to those who are elect exiles of the dispersion in Pontus, Galatia, Cappadocia, Asia, and Bithynia . . ." (1 Pet 1:1). Therefore, these instructions are not combatting a problem that is particular to one congregation. Rather, these instructions are addressed to multiple congregations throughout Asia Minor. Thus, Peter's instructions for wives to be subject to their husbands and for husbands to honor their wives follows the pattern of Paul's similar instructions since it is addressed to many churches spanning multiple regions. This, alongside the exegetical grounding in the patriarchal narrative, implies that Peter's instructions extend to all believers, not merely to a discrete time and social situation in the early church. Peter teaches a universal exegetical conclusion rather than a narrow response to one aberrant congregation.

In terms of the early audience, Clement of Alexandria understood 1 Peter 3:1–4 in this manner when he enjoined wives to win their unbelieving husbands through modesty and a meek and quiet spirit.[47] Tertullian and Cyprian each emphasized modesty in dress.[48] According to tradition, the apostolic teaching emphasized Sarah's example of showing honor to Abraham by calling him "lord" as an example for wives to honor their husband in marriage.[49] In his teaching on marriage, St. Augustine cites this passage in reference to wives winning their unbelieving husbands by good example, as well as believing husbands treating their wives well lest their prayers be hindered.[50]

47. Clement of Alexandria, *Instructor* 3.11 (*ANF* 2:287).

48. Tertullian, *Corona* 14 (*ANF* 3:102); Tertullian, *On Prayer* 20 (*ANF* 3:687); Cyprian, *Treatises* (*ANF* 5:432, 544).

49. *Constitutions of the Holy Apostles* 4.5.29 (ANF 7:463).

50. Augustine, *On the Good of Marriage* (*NPNF* 1.3:405); Augustine, *On the Good of Widowhood* (*NPNF* 1.3:443); Augustine, *On Marriage and Concupiscence* 1.10 (*NPNF* 1.5:267–68).

Summary and Conclusions

The Ethics of Creation
as Male and Female

THIS DISCUSSION BEGAN BY noting how the differentiated roles of men and women were established on day six of creation, which functions as the climax of the initial creation narrative in Genesis 1. This observation raises the prominence of ethical concerns associated with the differentiation of male and female at creation.[1] Moreover, the association of sexual differentiation with creation universalizes its ethics throughout all times and places. Early translations support the traditional interpretation of the Hebrew word normally rendered "help(er)" in Genesis 2:18–25, and the linguistic investigation of Walter Kaiser on this passage evidences serious methodological flaws both in terms of historical plausibility and methodological rigor. Second, although many egalitarians claim that role distinctions derive from the fall, we noted how Paul appeals to creation in Genesis 1–2 preceding the fall in 1 Corinthians 11:2–16, Ephesians 5:21–33, and at the beginning of his interpretation in 1 Timothy 2:12–15. Furthermore, the Petrine appeal to Sarah calling Abraham "lord" within the patriarchal narrative (1 Pet 3:1–7) casts her respect and submission toward Abraham as a redemption pattern for the elect. Thus, the grounding of apostolic

---

1. For applying the preceding exegesis, see Grudem and Rainey, eds., *Pastoral Leadership for Manhood and Womanhood*, as well as Köstenberger and Köstenberger, *God's Design for Man and Woman*.

exegesis in Torah provides further warrant for arguing this inspired interpretation of Scripture applies universally. The apostles declared inspired exegesis from the Mosaic covenant that was binding for the Christian covenant, and they were not merely reflecting the culture around them. This was not a sociologically driven response to specific churches, nor was this merely a codification of the cultural context in which the Bible was written. Therefore, one may legitimately conclude on sound hermeneutic principles that Pauline and Petrine scriptural instructions regarding the roles of men and women were intended for universal rather than local or historically discrete application. Moreover, these texts from two authors occur in epistolary material written to churches spanning Greece and Asia Minor. Thus, they are not limited to the social situation of one single community, as some would claim. The initial intended audiences of these instructions spanned a relatively large geographical area, and they were intended for circulation to multiple churches well into the future after their initial authorship and reception. Third, the examination of patristic exegesis and application bears out the early reception of this interpretation. A consideration of patristic citations in context indicates the church fathers remain the fountainhead of complementarian rather than egalitarian or feminist interpretation.

However, we did note the importance and the significance of the fall narrative in Genesis 3. First, the woman was deceived and the man followed her. Without thought or question, he failed to practice discernment as he passively followed in disobedience. Second, the man failed to protect his wife. He allowed her to enter into dialogue with the serpent, and then he unquestioningly followed her rather than reminding her of the command of the Lord God not to eat the fruit of the tree of the knowledge of good and evil. Third, the curse of the fall centers on the wrangling between man and woman, as well as the man exerting dominion over his wife in domineering fashion rather than cherishing the one who was created from the rib next to his heart. Therefore, redemption from the fall in Christian marriage and larger communal living does not mean the dissolution of role distinctions, but rather the sanctification of them. Anything less than man protecting and cherishing woman and woman helping man in submission and respect perpetuates the fall rather than reverses it. Egalitarians who conclude from unsanctified male abuse that all male leadership should therefore be abolished steer from the Scylla of man's brutal dominion into the Charybdis of woman's rebellion. The failure to apply Paul's principles for marriage from Ephesians 5:21–33 inhibits the spread of the glory of Christ through the witness of the church in family life, regardless of the rationales given. Moreover, the abdication of male leadership in the church, as with the ministries of Deborah in Judges 4–5 and Huldah in 2 Kings 22, presages judgment upon the church and a time of general exilic darkness in the absence of God.

Thus, the preceding discussion provides rational grounds for maintaining the traditional view of the scriptural roles of men and women. These are the views handed down by the apostles, and they remain universally binding through time. It is the author's sincere prayer that the remnant will be encouraged, and those who disagree will wrestle with this issue further in order to break with the spirit of the age. As Paul wrote,

> the Lord's servant must not be quarrelsome but kind to everyone, able to teach, patiently enduring evil, correcting his opponents with gentleness. God may perhaps grant them repentance leading to a knowledge of the truth, and they may escape from the snare of the devil, after being captured by him to do his will. (2 Tim 2:24–26)

Bibliography

Ambrose. *Dogmatic Treatises, Ethical Works, and Sermons.* In *NPNF* ser. 1, vol. 10.

———. *Exposition of the Christian Faith.* In *NPNF* ser. 1, vol. 10.

Augustine. *Confessions.* In *NPNF* ser. 1, vol. 1.

———. *Lectures or Tractates on the Gospel According to St. John Chapter XVII.21–23.* In *NPNF* ser. 1, vol. 7.

———. *On Continence.* In *NPNF* ser. 1, vol. 3.

———. *On Genesis.* Hyde Park, NY: New City, 2002.

———. *On the Good of Marriage.* In *NPNF* ser. 1, vol. 3.

———. *On the Good of Widowhood.* In *NPNF* ser. 1, vol. 3.

———. *On the Holy Trinity.* In *NPNF* ser. 1, vol. 3.

———. *On Marriage and Concupiscence.* In *NPNF* ser. 1, vol. 5.

———. *Our Lord's Sermon on the Mount.* In *NPNF* ser. 1, vol. 6.

———. *Sermons on Selected Lessons of the New Testament.* In *NPNF* ser. 1, vol. 6.

———. *Writings in Connection with the Manichaean Controversy: Reply to Faustus the Manichaean.* In *NPNF* ser. 1, vol. 4.

Barrett, Matthew. "God's Design for Marriage: Celebrating the Beauty of Gender Roles in 1 Peter 3." *JBMW* 20.1 (2015). https://cbmw.org/2015/05/27/from-the-sacred-desk-gods-design-for-marriage-celebrating-the-beauty-of-gender-roles-in-1-peter-31-7/.

Bauer, Walter, F. W. Danker, W. F. Arndt, and F. W. Gingrich. *A Greek-English Lexicon of the New Testament and other Early Christian Literature.* 3rd ed. Chicago: University of Chicago, 1999.

Baugh, S. M. "A Foreign World: Ephesus in the First Century." In *Women in the Church,* edited by Köstenberger and Schreiner, 13–38. 1995. Reprint, Grand Rapids: Baker, 2005.

Baumgardner, Jennifer, and Amy Richards. *Manifesta: Young Women, Feminism, and the Future.* New York: Farrar, Straus and Giroux, 2000.

Belleville, Linda L. "Teaching and Usurping Authority: 1 Timothy 2:11–15." In *Discovering Biblical Equality: Complementarity Without Hierarchy,* edited by Ronald W. Pierce and Rebecca Merrill Groothuis, 205–23. Downers Grove, IL: InterVarsity, 2004.

———. "Women Leaders in the Bible." In *Discovering Biblical Equality: Complementarity Without Hierarchy*, edited by Ronald W. Pierce and Rebecca Merrill Groothuis, 111–15. Downers Grove, IL: InterVarsity, 2004.

Bilezikian, Gilbert. *Beyond Sex Roles: What the Bible Says about a Woman's Place in Church and Family*. 3rd ed. Grand Rapids: Baker Academic, 2006.

Bordwine, James E. *The Pauline Doctrine of Male Headship: The Apostle Versus Biblical Feminists*. Vancouver, BC: Westminster Institute, 1996.

Brown, J. G. "A Historian Looks at 1 Timothy 2:11–14." *Priscilla Papers* 26.3 (2012). https://www.cbeinternational.org/resource/article/priscilla-papers-academic-journal/historian-looks-1-timothy-211–14.

———. "What About Deborah?" *Priscilla Papers* 28.3 (2014). https://www.cbeinternational.org/resource/article/priscilla-papers-academic-journal/what-about-deborah.

Byrd, Aimee. *Recovering from Biblical Manhood and Womanhood: How the Church Needs to Rediscover Her Purpose*. Grand Rapids: Zondervan Academic, 2020.

Calvin, John. *Genesis*. Translated by Rev. John King. 1847. Calvin's Commentaries. Reprint, Grand Rapids: Baker, 1998.

Carson, D. A. "'Silent in the Churches': On the Role of Women in 1 Corinthians 14:33b–36." In *Recovering Biblical Manhood and Womanhood: A Response to Evangelical Feminism*, edited by John Piper and Wayne Grudem, 140–53. 1991. Reprint, Wheaton, IL: Crossway, 2006.

Cassuto, Umberto. *A Commentary on the Book of Genesis. Part 1, from Adam to Noah*. 1944. Translated by Israel Abrahams. Jerusalem: Magnes, 1961.

Cervin, Richard S. "Does *Kephalē* Mean 'Source' or 'Authority' in Greek Literature? A Rebuttal." *Trinity Journal* 10, n.s. (1989) 85–112.

———. "On the Significance of *Kephalē* ("Head"): A Study of the Abuse of One Greek Word." *Priscilla Papers* 30.2 (2016). https://www.cbeinternational.org/resource/article/priscilla-papers-academic-journal/significance-kephale-head-study-abuse-one-greek.

Chrysostom, John. *A Commentary on the Acts of the Apostles*. In *NPNF* ser. 1, vol. 11.

———. *Homilies on Colossians*. In *NPNF* ser. 1, vol. 13.

———. *Homilies on Ephesians*. In *NPNF* ser. 1, vol. 13.

———. *Homilies on First Corinthians*. In *NPNF* ser. 1, vol. 12.

———. *Homilies on First Timothy*. In *NPNF* ser. 1, vol. 13.

———. *Homilies on Paul's Epistles to the Romans on Rom xiii.1*. In *NPNF* ser. 1, vol. 11.

———. *Homilies on Titus*. In *NPNF* ser. 1, vol. 13.

———. *Treatise Concerning the Christian Priesthood*. In *NPNF* ser. 1, vol. 9.

Clement of Alexandria. *Exhortation to the Heathen*. In *ANF* vol. 2.

———. *Homilies*. In *ANF* vol. 2.

———. *The Instructor*. In *ANF* vol. 2.

———. *The Stromata*. In *ANF* vol. 2.

Corley, Kathleen. *Women and the Historical Jesus: Feminist Myths of Christian Origins*. Santa Rosa, CA: Polebridge, 2002.

Constitutions of the Holy Apostles. In *ANF* vol. 7.

Croteau, David. "'To Make Her Holy' (Ephesians 5:26): Are Husbands Responsible for the Spiritual Maturation of Their Wives?" *JBMW* 21.1 (2016). https://cbmw.org/2016/05/16/jbmw-21-1-to-make-her-holy-ephesians-526-are-husbands-responsible-for-the-spiritual-maturation-of-their-wives/.

Cyprian. *Treatises*. In *ANF* vol. 5.

Cyril. *Procatechesis*. In *NPNF* ser. 2, vol. 7.

Davids, Peter H. "A Silent Witness in Marriage: 1 Peter 3:1–7." In *Discovering Biblical Equality: Complementarity Without Hierarchy*, edited by Ronald W. Pierce and Rebecca Merrill Groothuis, 224–38. Downers Grove, IL: InterVarsity, 2004.

Davis, John Jefferson. "Incarnation, Trinity, and the Ordination of Women to the Priesthood." *Priscilla Papers* 24.1 (2010). https://www.cbeinternational.org/resource/article/priscilla-papers-academic-journal/incarnation-trinity-and-ordination-women.

DeRouchie, Jason S. "Confronting the Transgender Storm: New Covenant Reflections on Deuteronomy 22:5." *JBMW* 21.1 (2016). https://cbmw.org/2016/05/25/jbmw-21-1-confronting-the-transgender-storm-new-covenant-reflections-from-deuteronomy-225/.

Driver, S. R. *The Book of Genesis: With Introduction and Notes*. 7th ed. London: Methuen, 1909.

Elliott, John H. "Jesus Was Not an Egalitarian: A Critique of the Anachronistic and Idealist Theory." *BTB* 32 (2002) 75–91.

———. "The Jesus Movement Was Not Egalitarian but Family-Oriented." *BibInt* 11.2 (2003) 173–210.

Fee, Gordon D. "The Cultural Context of Ephesians 5:18—6:9." *Priscilla Papers* 33.4 (2017). https://www.cbeinternational.org/resource/article/priscilla-papers-academic-journal/cultural-context-ephesians-518-69-0.

———. "Male and Female in the New Creation: Galatians 3:26–29." In *Discovering Biblical Equality: Complementarity Without Hierarchy*, edited by Ronald W. Pierce and Rebecca Merrill Groothuis, 172–85. Downers Grove, IL: InterVarsity, 2004.

———. "Praying and Prophesying in the Assemblies." In *Discovering Biblical Equality: Complementarity Without Hierarchy*, edited by Ronald W. Pierce and Rebecca Merrill Groothuis, 142–60. Downers Grove, IL: InterVarsity, 2004.

Foster, Tim. "1 Timothy 2:8–15 and Gender Wars at Ephesus." *Priscilla Papers* 30.3 (2016). https://www.cbeinternational.org/resource/article/priscilla-papers-academic-journal/1-timothy-28-15-and-gender-wars-ephesus.

Frame, John M. *The Doctrine of the Christian Life*. A Theology of Lordship. Phillipsburg: P&R, 2008.

Bibliography

Gabrielle, Haley. "Kephalē as Fountainhead in 1 Corinthians 11:3." *Priscilla Papers* 32.3 (2018). https://www.cbeinternational.org/resources/article/priscilla-papers/.

Gentry, Peter J. "Humanity as the Divine Image in Genesis 1:26–28." *Eikon* 2.1 (2020) 56–69. https://cbmw.org/2020/06/10/humanity-as-the-divine-image-in-genesis-126-28/.

Gesenius, W., E. Kautzsch, and A. E. Cowley. *Gesenius' Hebrew Grammar*. 2nd. ed. Oxford: Clarendon, 1910.

Giles, Kevin. "The Genesis of Confusion." *Priscilla Papers* 29.1 (2015). https://www.cbeinternational.org/resource/article/priscilla-papers-academic-journal/genesis-confusion.

————. "The Genesis of Equality, Part 1." *Priscilla Papers* 28.4 (2014). https://www.cbeinternational.org/resource/article/priscilla-papers-academic-journal/genesis-equality-part-1.

Gregory of Nazianzus. "On the Death of His Father." In *Select Orations*, in *NPNF* ser. 2, vol. 7.

Groothuis, Rebecca Merrill. *The Feminist Bogeywoman: Questions and Answers about Evangelical Feminism*. Grand Rapids: Baker, 1995.

————. *Good News for Women: A Biblical Picture of Gender Equality*. Grand Rapids: Baker, 1997.

————. *Women Caught in the Conflict: The Culture War between Traditionalism and Feminism*. Grand Rapids: Baker, 1994.

Grudem, Wayne, ed. *Biblical Foundations for Manhood and Womanhood*. Wheaton, IL: Crossway, 2002.

————. *Christian Ethics: An Introduction to Biblical Moral Reasoning*. Wheaton, IL: Crossway, 2018.

————. *Countering the Claims of Evangelical Feminism*. Colorado Springs, CO: Multnomah, 2006.

————. "Does *Kephalē* ('Head') Mean 'Source' or 'Authority Over' in Greek Literature? A Survey of 2,336 Examples." *Trinity Journal* 6, n.s. (1985) 38–59. Reprinted in George W. Knight, *The Role Relationship of Men and Women: New Testament Teaching*, 49–80. Rev. ed. Chicago: Moody, 1985.

————. *Evangelical Feminism: A New Path to Liberalism?* Wheaton, IL: Crossway, 2006.

————. *Evangelical Feminism and Biblical Truth: An Analysis of More Than One Hundred Disputed Questions*. Sisters, OR: Multnomah, 2004.

————. "Wives Like Sarah, and the Husbands Who Honor Them: 1 Peter 3:1–7." In *Recovering Biblical Manhood and Womanhood: A Response to Evangelical Feminism*, edited by John Piper and Wayne Grudem, 194–208. 1991. Reprint, Wheaton, IL: Crossway, 2006.

Grudem, Wayne, and Dennis Rainey, eds. *Pastoral Leadership for Manhood and Womanhood*. Wheaton, IL: Crossway, 2002.

Gunkel, H. *Genesis*. 5th ed. GHAT 1. Göttingen: Vandenhoeck & Ruprecht, 1922.

Bibliography

Hall, Jason, and Peter R. Schemm Jr. "Marriage as It Was Meant to Be Seen: Headship, Submission, and the Gospel." *JBMW* 15.1 (2010) 13–14.

Harris, Joshua. "A Word to Husbands (and a Few More for Wives): 1 Peter 3:1–7." *JBMW* 16.1(2011) 34–39.

Hassey, Janette Hassey. *No Time for Silence: Evangelical Women in Public Ministry Around the Turn of the Century.* Grand Rapids: Zondervan, 1986.

Hess, Richard S. "Equality With and Without Innocence." In *Discovering Biblical Equality: Complementarity Without Hierarchy*, edited by Ronald W. Pierce and Rebecca Merrill Groothuis, 96–109. Downers Grove, IL: InterVarsity, 2004.

Hübner, Jamin. "Revisiting the Clarity of Scripture in 1 Timothy 2:12." *Priscilla Papers* 30.3 (2016). https://www.cbe.org.au/index.php/biblical-studies/153-revisiting-the-clarity-of-scripture-in-1-timothy-2-12.

———. "Translating Αὐθεντέω (Authenteō) in 1 Timothy 2:12a." *Priscilla Papers* 29.2 (2015). https://www.cbeinternational.org/resource/article/priscilla-papers-academic-journal/translating-aythenteo-authenteo-1-timothy-212a.

Hung, Eugene. "Defending My Daughters Against Rape Culture." *Mutuality* 24.1 (2017). https://www.cbeinternational.org/resource/article/mutuality-blog-magazine/defending-my-daughters-against-rape-culture.

Hunt, Mary E., and Diann L. Neu, eds. *New Feminist Christianity: Many Voices, Many Views.* Woodstock, VT: Skylight Paths, 2010.

Hunt, Susan. "Women's Ministry in the Local Church: A Covenantal and Complementarian Approach." *JBMW* 11.2 (2006) 37–47.

Hyppolytus. *The Refutation of All Heresies.* In *ANF* vol. 5.

Ignatius. *Epistle to the Philadelphians.* In *ANF* vol. 1.

Jerome. *Letter LXXV to Theodora.* In *NPNF* ser. 2, vol. 6.

———. *To Principia.* In *NPNF* ser. 2, vol. 6.

Jewett, Paul K. *Man as Male and Female: A Study in Sexual Relationships from a Theological Point of View.* Grand Rapids: Eerdmans, 1975.

———. *The Ordination of Women: An Essay on the Office of Christian Ministry.* Grand Rapids: Eerdmans, 1980.

Joüon, Paul, and T. Muraoka. *A Grammar of Biblical Hebrew.* 2 vols. Subsidia Biblica 14/I. Rome: Pontificio Istituto Biblico, 2003.

Kaiser, Walter. "Correcting Caricatures: The Biblical Teaching on Women." *Priscilla Papers* 19.2/30.4 (2005/2019). https://www.cbeinternational.org/resource/article/priscilla-papers-academic-journal/correcting-caricatures.

———. "Paul, Women and the Church." *Worldwide Challenge*, September 1976, 9–12.

Kassian, Mary. "A Review of Ruth A. Tucker 'Black and White Bible, Black and Blue Wife.'" May 13, 2016. https://cbmw.org/book-reviews-3/a-review-of-ruth-a-tucker-black-and-white-bible-black-and-blue-wife/.

Keener, Craig S. "Learning in the Assemblies: 1 Corinthians 14:34–35." In *Discovering Biblical Equality: Complementarity Without Hierarchy*, edited

Bibliography

by Ronald W. Pierce and Rebecca Merrill Groothuis, 161–71. Downers Grove, IL: InterVarsity, 2004.

Keil, C. F., and F. Delitzsch. *Commentary on the Old Testament.* 1866–91. 10 vols. Reprint, Peabody, MA: Hendrickson, 1996.

Kidd, Sue Monk. *The Dance of the Dissident Daughter: A Woman's Journey from Christian Tradition to the Sacred Feminine.* New York: HarperCollins, 1996.

Knight, George W., III. "Husbands and Wives as Analogues of Christ and the Church: Ephesians 5:21–33 and Colossians 3:18–19." In *Recovering Biblical Manhood and Womanhood: A Response to Evangelical Feminism*, edited by John Piper and Wayne Grudem, 165–78. 1991. Reprint, Wheaton, IL: Crossway, 2006.

———. *The Role Relationship of Men and Women: New Testament Teaching.* Rev. ed. Chicago: Moody, 1985.

Koehler, Ludwig, Walter Baumgartner, and Johann Jakob Stamm. *The Hebrew and Aramaic Lexicon of the Old Testament.* Translated and edited by M. E. J. Richardson. 2 vols. Leiden: Brill, 2001.

Köstenberger, Andreas J. "The Syntax of 1 Timothy 2:12: A Rejoinder to Philip B. Payne." *JBMW* 14.2 (2009) 37–40.

Köstenberger, Andreas J., and Margaret E. Köstenberger. *God's Design for Man and Woman: A Biblical and Theological Survey.* Wheaton, IL: Crossway, 2014.

Köstenberger, Andreas J., and Thomas R. Schreiner, eds. *Women in the Church: An Analysis and Application of 1 Timothy 2:9–15.* 2nd ed. Grand Rapids: Baker Academic, 2005.

Kroeger, Richard Clark, and Catherine Clark Kroeger. *I Suffer Not a Woman: Rethinking 1 Timothy 2:11–15 in Light of Ancient Evidence.* Grand Rapids: Baker, 1992.

Lewis, C. S. "On the Reading of Old Books." In *God in the Dock: Essays on Theology and Ethics*, edited by Walter Hooper, 200–207. Grand Rapids: Eerdmans, 1970.

———. "Priestesses in the Church?" In *God in the Dock: Essays on Theology and Ethics*, edited by Walter Hooper, 234–39. Grand Rapids: Eerdmans, 1970.

MacGregor, Kirk. "1 Corinthians 14:33b–38 as a Pauline Quotation-Refutation Device." *Priscilla Papers* 32.1 (2018). https://www.cbeinternational.org/resource/article/priscilla-papers-academic-journal/1-corinthians-1433b-38-pauline-quotation.

Marshall, I. Howard. "Mutual Love and Submission in Marriage: Colossians 3:18–19 and Ephesians 5:21–33." In *Discovering Biblical Equality: Complementarity Without Hierarchy*, edited by Ronald W. Pierce and Rebecca Merrill Groothuis, 186–204. Downers Grove, IL: InterVarsity, 2004.

McCulley, Carolyn. "When You Don't Have a Better Half: Encouraging Biblical Roles as a Single Woman." *JBMW* 11.2 (2006) 69–75.

Bibliography

McKnight, Scot. *The Blue Parakeet: Rethinking How You Read the Bible*. Grand Rapids: Zondervan, 2008.

Methodius. *The Banquet of the Ten Virgins*. In *ANF* vol. 6.

Mickelsen, Berkeley, and Alvera Mickelsen. "Does Male Dominance Tarnish Our Translations?" *Christianity Today*, October 5, 1979, 23–29.

———. "The 'Head' of the Epistles." *Christianity Today*, February 20, 1981, 20–23.

Miller, Becky Castle. "Misinterpreting 'Head' Can Perpetuate Abuse." *Mutuality* 24.4 (2017). https://www.cbeinternational.org/resources/article/mutuality/misinterpreting-head-can-perpetuate-abuse.

Mollenkott, Virginia Ramey. *Women, Men, and the Bible*. Rev. ed. New York: Crossroad, 1988.

Moo, Douglas. "What Does It Mean Not to Teach or Have Authority over Men? 1 Timothy 2:11–15." In *Recovering Biblical Manhood and Womanhood: A Response to Evangelical Feminism*, edited by John Piper and Wayne Grudem, 179–93. 1991. Reprint, Wheaton, IL: Crossway, 2006.

Moore, Russell D. "O.J. Simpson Is Not a Complementarian: Male Headship and Violence against Women." *JBMW* 12.1 (2007) 2–6.

———. "Women, Stop Submitting to Men." *JBMW* 17.1(2012) 8–9.

Murphy, Edwina, and David I Starling, eds. *The Gender Conversation: Evangelical Perspectives on Gender, Scripture, and the Christian Life*. Eugene, OR: Wipf and Stock, 2016.

Naselli, Andrew David. "Does Anyone Need to Recover from Biblical Manhood and Womanhood?" Review of Aimee Byrd's *Recovering from Biblical Manhood and Womanhood*. *Eikon* 2.1 (2020) 109–51. https://cbmw.org/2020/05/04/does-anyone-need-to-recover-from-biblical-manhood-and-womanhood-a-review-article-of-aimee-byrds-recovering-from-biblical-manhood-and-womanhood/.

Nugent, John. "The 'Weaker Sex' or a Weak Translation? Strengthening Our Interpretation of 1 Peter 3:7." *Priscilla Papers* 32.3 (2018). https://www.cbeinternational.org/resource/article/priscilla-papers-academic-journal/weaker-sex-or-weak-translation-strengthening-our.

Ortlund, Jani. "Sweet Sacrifices: The Challenges of a Woman in Ministry." *JBMW* 14.1 (2009) 22–28.

Parnell, Jonathan, and Owen Strachan, eds. *Designed for Joy: How the Gospel Impacts Men and Women, Identity and Practice*. Wheaton, IL: Crossway, 2015.

Payne, Philip B. *Man and Woman, One in Christ: An Exegetical and Theological Study of Paul's Letters*. Grand Rapids: Zondervan, 2009.

Peppiatt, Lucy. *Women and Worship at Corinth: Paul's Rhetorical Arguments in 1 Corinthians*. Eugene, OR: Cascade, 2015.

Pierce, Ronald W. "Deborah: Troublesome Woman or Woman of Valor?" *Priscilla Papers* 32.2 (2018). https://www.cbeinternational.org/resource/article/priscilla-papers-academic-journal/deborah-troublesome-woman-or-woman-valor.

Bibliography

———. *Partners in Marriage & Ministry: A Biblical Picture of Gender Equality.* Minneapolis: Christians for Biblical Equality, 2011.

Pierce, Ronald W., and Rebecca Merrill Groothuis, eds. *Discovering Biblical Equality: Complementarity without Hierarchy.* Downers Grove, IL: InterVarsity, 2005.

Pierre, Jeremy Pierre. "An Overlooked Help: Church Discipline and the Protection of Women." *JBMW* 18.1(2013) 12–15.

Piper, John. "Clarifying Words on Wife Abuse." *JBMW* 18.1(2013) 10–11.

Piper, John, and Wayne Grudem, eds. *Recovering Biblical Manhood and Womanhood: A Response to Evangelical Feminism.* 1991. Reprint, Wheaton: Crossway, 2006.

Rad, Gerhard von. *Genesis.* Translated by John H. Marks. Rev. ed. OTL. Philadelphia: Westminster, 1972.

Riswold, Caryn D. *Feminism and Christianity: Questions and Answers in the Third Wave.* Eugene, OR: Cascade, 2009.

Rosner, Brian S. *Paul, Scripture and Ethics: A Study of 1 Corinthians 5–7.* AGJU 22. Leiden: Brill, 1994.

Ruether, Rosemary Radford. *Gaia and God: An Ecofeminist Theology of Earth Healing.* New York: HarperCollins, 1992.

———. *Goddesses and the Divine Feminine.* Berkeley: University of California Press, 2005.

———. *Sexism and God-Talk: Toward a Feminist Theology.* 1983. Reprint, Boston: Beacon, 1993.

———. *Womanguides: Readings toward a Feminist Theology.* Boston: Beacon, 1996.

Scanzoni, Letha Dawson, and Nancy A. Hardesty. *All We're Meant to Be: Biblical Feminism for Today.* 1974. Reprint, Grand Rapids: Eerdmans, 1992.

Schreiner, Thomas R. "Head Coverings, Prophecies, and the Trinity: 1 Corinthians 11:2–16." In *Recovering Biblical Manhood and Womanhood: A Response to Evangelical Feminism,* edited by John Piper and Wayne Grudem, 124–39. 1991. Reprint, Wheaton, IL: Crossway, 2006.

Schüssler Fiorenza, Elisabeth. *Bread Not Stone: The Challenge of Feminist Biblical Interpretation.* Boston: Beacon, 1995.

———. *But She Said: Feminist Practices of Biblical Interpretation.* Boston: Beacon, 1992.

———. *In Memory of Her: A Feminist Theological Reconstruction of Christian Origins.* New York: Crossroad, 1994.

———. *Wisdom Ways: Introducing Feminist Biblical Interpretation.* Maryknoll, NY: Orbis, 2001.

Spencer, Aida Besançon. *Beyond the Curse: Women Called to Ministry.* 1985. Grand Rapids: Baker, 2010.

———, ed. *The Goddess Revival.* Grand Rapids: Baker, 1995.

Spencer, Aida Besançon, William David Spencer, and Mimi Haddad. *Global Voices on Biblical Equality: Women and Men Ministering Together in the Church.* Eugene, OR: Wipf and Stock, 2008.

Bibliography

Strachan, Owen, and Gavin Peacock. *The Grand Design: Male and Female He Made Them*. Fearn, Ross-shire: Christian Focus, 2016.

Tertullian. *De Corona*. In *ANF* vol. 3.

———. *The Five Books against Marcion*. In *ANF* vol. 3.

———. *On Baptism*. In *ANF* vol. 3.

———. *On Prayer*. In *ANF* vol. 3.

———. *On the Veiling of Virgins*. In *ANF* vol. 4.

Thiselton, Anthony. *The First Epistle to the Corinthians: A Commentary on the Greek Text*. NIGTC. Grand Rapids: Eerdmans, 2000.

Tomson, Peter J. *Paul and the Jewish Law: Halakha in the Letters of the Apostle to the Gentiles*. Assen: Van Gorcum, 1990.

Trible, Phyllis. *God and the Rhetoric of Sexuality*. OBT. Philadelphia: Fortress, 1978.

———. *Texts of Terror: Literary-Feminist Readings of Biblical Narratives*. OBT. Minneapolis: Fortress, 1994.

Tucker, Ruth A. *Black and White Bible, Black and Blue Wife: My Story of Finding Hope after Domestic Abuse*. Grand Rapids: Zondervan, 2016.

———. *Dynamic Women of the Bible: What We Can Learn from Their Surprising Stories*. Grand Rapids: Baker, 2014.

———. *Women in the Maze: Questions and Answers on Biblical Equality*. Downers Grove, IL: InterVarsity, 1992.

Walden, Wayne. "Galatians 3:28: Grammar, Text, Context, and Translation." *JBMW* 15.1 (2010) 23–26.

Waltke, Bruce, and M. O'Connor. *An Introduction to Biblical Hebrew Syntax*. Winona Lake, IN: Eisenbrauns, 1990.

Warfield, B. B. *Revelation and Inspiration*. Works of Benjamin B. Warfield 1. 1932. Reprint, Grand Rapids: Baker, 2003.

Webb, William J. *Slaves, Women and Homosexuals: Exploring the Hermeneutics of Cultural Analysis*. Downers Grove, IL: InterVarsity, 2001.

Wenham, Gordon J. *Genesis 1–15*. WBC 1. Nashville: T. Nelson, 1987.

Westermann, Claus. *Genesis 1–11*. 1974. Translated by John J. Scullion. CC. Minneapolis: Fortress, 1994.

Witherington, Ben, III. *Paul's Narrative Thought World: The Tapestry of Tragedy and Triumph*. Louisville: Westminster/John Knox, 1994.

Wolters, Albert. "A Semantic Study of αὐθέντης and Its Derivatives." *JBMW* 11.1 (2006) 44–65.

Zlotowitz, Rabbi Meir (trans. and comment.), and Rabbi Nosson Scherman (overviews). *Bereishis* (ספר בראשית) *Genesis: A New Translation with a Commentary Anthologized from Talmudic, Midrashic and Rabbinic Sources*. Artscroll Ta'anach. New York: Mesorah, 1977.

www.ingramcontent.com/pod-product-compliance
Lightning Source LLC
Chambersburg PA
CBHW060425090426
42734CB00011B/2449